Plus More Life:
A #HeartStrong Story

A Survivor's Journey of Heart, Humor, Healing, and Health

SAM "SP" PREWITT

Cool and Creative Concepts LLC

To the Many I Heart,

For the Few Close to My Heart,

And for the One Who Has My Heart...

I do this for you.

Above all else, guard your heart, for everything you do flows from it.

— **Proverbs 4:23 (NIV)**

Contents

Introduction

"**S**ir, we do not even know how you are alive."

Those were the words that made death feel real to me. We all hear about it or see family and friends go through it, but you are never ready when it comes knocking at your door. Hearing those words made me look hard at the life I had lived up to that moment. What am I doing today? What am I doing with this second chance while I still have the power to shape my own legacy?

Hi, my name is Sam. I come from a good, loving family, a tight-knit community that taught me to value connection. Some say I've never met a stranger. I've always made it my mission to make people feel at home, encouraged, and seen even before I truly understood why it mattered.

Radio was my calling: nearly a decade behind the mic and in the boardroom, living my dream. I was surrounded by friends, thriving in my career, believing I had everything figured out and nothing left to prove.

But God had another chapter waiting. To show me my true purpose, I had to nearly lose the one thing I took most for granted, my life. I had to learn the hard way just how precious a second chance really is.

At the age of twenty-nine, I suffered a massive heart attack, and according to the doctors, I shouldn't have walked out of that hospital. The hardest truth? It could have been prevented. I brushed off warning signs, ignored diagnoses, and comforted myself by thinking, *These things just run in the family.* I felt almost reassured knowing others shared those generational issues.

It felt as though all the adults around me listed their health ailments as badges of honor, many of them bonding over similar health diagnoses. So, upon hearing my own diagnosis at thirteen years old, though I was young, I felt it was inevitable. I assumed that health issues are just a result of eating some of the foods that are considered "bad." But the tastes, smells, and memories associated with these foods were worth it—until the day they weren't.

I still remember lying in that hospital bed, watching the ceiling tiles, every beep of the monitor a reminder of how fragile life really is. Each breath felt like both a question and an answer: Could I keep going? Would I get to see another day, another chance to love, to laugh, to grow? Those walls became my early classroom for learning that life isn't guaranteed, but every moment is precious.

What surprised me most was the steady stream of visitors I received during my hospital stay. People from every part of my life showed up, surrounding me with love and support. Those visits opened my eyes to how big my tribe truly is and how deeply people care about me. Their love and appreciation made me realize that protecting myself and fighting for my health is not just about me; it's about being here for the people who love me so we can continue making memories, growing, and laughing together.

Maybe you've brushed off your own warning signs. Maybe you've told yourself, "That's just how it is" about things that run in your family. Maybe you come from a background or a generation where silence feels safer than facing up to hard truths. But I promise you that silence nearly cost me everything.

Most people would keep a story like mine private. But I feel called to share for one simple reason: I care. My story isn't about fear, pity, or guilt. It's about honesty. More than anything, it's about saving others from the path I almost couldn't come back from.

I've told my story hundreds of times at health events and in intimate gatherings, and the reactions are almost always the same: shock, intrigue, and inspiration. I know my story is powerful, but telling it one-on-one or to small crowds is only the beginning. To truly raise awareness about the #HeartStrong mission, to encourage people to take care of themselves so they can stick around for their own best moments, and, if I'm honest, to help save lives, I wrote this book.

Here's what I want you to know: The best years of my life have come after my heart attack. Recovery didn't just give me back my days—it made every minute mean more. From advancing my career to building a family and collecting once-in-a-lifetime experiences, I've discovered you really can control your outcome, break generational curses, and not just survive but thrive. If I can, so can you.

In these pages, you'll find hard truths, learned lessons, and the practical tools that helped me change from the inside out. You'll meet the people who kept me accountable, the routines that restored my hope, and the moments—big and small—that taught me to love my life all over again.

I don't preach. I don't shame. Those approaches never worked for me, and I don't expect them to work for you. I just tell it as it is—so my mistakes don't become your fate. Life is too precious not to fight for it. That's the heart of the #HeartStrong movement: *protecting your heart and everything in it.*

If you take anything from this book, let it be this: You matter. Your heart matters—literally and figuratively. And there are people—like me—rooting for you to beat the odds and build a legacy only you can build.

Let's begin this journey.

I

"You Won't Live to See Thirty"

Let's start with a breathing exercise. Close your eyes and take a deep breath. After a few seconds, exhale fully. It feels good, doesn't it? There's nothing like the euphoric feeling of air as it passes through your nose, down your throat, and into your lungs. Notice your heart beating more slowly within your chest, your body calming, and any stress melting away. We'll explore more breathing exercises later, but for now, let me take you back to 1999.

The year 1999 was packed with memorable moments: Cash Money Records taking over for the '99 and the 2000, Pokémon cards flooding playgrounds, and Lauryn Hill winning five Grammys—including Album of the Year, the first hip-hop album ever to win that award—for *The Miseducation of Lauryn Hill,* Tiger Woods' first PGA Championship, and *The Matrix* "red pill or blue pill" debate. Then came the Y2K apocalypse buzz—people everywhere were convinced computers would crash at midnight on January 1, 2000. Prince's "1999" played on repeat, sounding more like a warning than a party anthem.

But for me, 1999 will always have a different meaning. That was the year I first heard I had high cholesterol. At thirteen, I had no idea what that even meant, and I never stopped to ask. I certainly didn't know it could lead to heart attacks or strokes. At that age, I just didn't care. I was too young, too wrapped up in making sure I didn't get in trouble at school, trying to finish my homework and chores before running outside to play.

Even after my diagnosis, I didn't stop eating fast food or all the amazing soul food my grandmother and mother would cook. All I wanted was to be like my friends, to keep eating the foods I loved without worry. Worst of all, I wasn't on any medication. In my mother's eyes, I was way too young for that. She didn't want me on medicine so early in life.

Looking back, I hate that I didn't care. I figured none of it would matter until I got to my dad's age, which to my young eyes seemed "old," since that's when I saw him dealing with most of his heart issues. My mother did what she could to help me avoid his fate, but my own ignorance and refusal to take things seriously eventually caught up to me.

Let's take a break here for another breathing exercise.

This time, I want you to picture something: As you breathe in, the air moves in much more slowly, as if something is blocking it. Every breath feels incomplete, like you can't quite fill your lungs, making you anxious and searching for relief that never comes. Your heart beats faster and harder. Yet your brain insists that everything is fine.

That's what my heart attack felt like.

It's not always what you think it will be. We've been told for years that your arm goes numb and an elephant sits on your chest. Sometimes that happens. But sometimes, like for me at twenty-nine, none of the symptoms are "typical."

I titled this chapter "You Won't Live to See Thirty" for a reason. I still remember being at the doctor's office for my seasonal allergies, just wanting some medicine, when she looked at my labs and said, "I've never seen cholesterol numbers like these in someone your age." I was only twenty-six years old at the time. I brushed it off, feeling a little judged. I was wrong.

Before I explain my missteps, let's take one last deep breath: in through your nose, hold for a second, and release through your mouth. Feels great, right? Now, let's begin. Let me take you back to where this story really starts—with my family.

2

Sweet Home Alabama

Prewitt Pride and Jenkins Joy

The sweltering summer heat, the unforgettable red dirt that seemed endless, and the delicious Southern home cooking are how I remember my parents' birthplace, Northport, Alabama. Our family would frequent the South, as they loved returning home from Ohio to see family. To get back to the South, we would drive.

The drive was twelve hours long. My father always drove, with my mother in the front seat. My two sisters and I were in the back seat, and I was always the one in the middle. There were no cell phones or portable entertainment devices. But there were snacks.

We would keep cold sandwiches and soda pop in the cooler for when we got hungry. My father didn't like stopping; the goal was to get home. We only got a break when we hit our rest stops in Tennessee and Kentucky. We would take bathroom breaks and sometimes get a meal. The only way to pass the time was to go to sleep. I knew if I took about three naps, it would make the twelve-hour trip feel much shorter.

Whenever I saw the space shuttle in Huntsville, Alabama, I knew we were close and that I had a chance to get one more nap in. Before I knew it, we'd pull up my grandmother's narrow driveway and be greeted by Grandma and Grandpa, who always seemed to know our arrival time to the second. Being greeted with that amount of love made those twelve hours worthwhile.

The trips back to Alabama allowed me to spend quality time with my family, especially my grandparents. They were much older, so time was limited. Thankfully, I spent over thirty years with my grandmother and grandfather. The time was used wisely, as I learned a lot about our family, traditions, and family health history.

Knowing your family history is essential. According to the National Institutes of Health's National Library of Medicine, your family genes, environment, lifestyle, and habits are some of the strongest influences on your risk of developing heart disease, diabetes, or cancer, or experiencing a stroke. While you can't change your genes, being aware of potential health issues and catching them early can help reduce your risk. A simple place to start is with your family's origins.

Northport is located right next to Tuscaloosa, near the University of Alabama. My parents were both born in the Jim Crow South in 1950. My mother, Alfreda Jenkins, is the youngest of three born to Emmanuel Jenkins Jr. and Gussie Mae Jenkins. My father, Sam Edward Prewitt, is a key character in this story. He was born to a man named Mr. Morrow and Betty Mae Steele. Mr. Morrow fathered him, but he wasn't his dad. My father was raised by Sam Prewitt, who married my grandmother and raised my father as his own.

You may be wondering if I am Sam Prewitt III. While we share the same first and last names, we each have different middle names. Upon marriage, my grandmother also adopted this surname. My father was the oldest of five, growing up with two brothers and two sisters. He was born five minutes from the suburban side of Northport, where my mother lived, in an area called the Valley.

My parents missed their hometown so much that sometimes they would pick me up from school and we'd hit the road back to Alabama just for the weekend. The twelve-hour drive was second nature to them. Most people wouldn't think it was worth the long drive for such a short time, but that never stopped them. Family was everything, so the trips were always worth it.

Back home in Alabama, my mother would spend time with her parents. Being the youngest, she was always close to them. Even when she wasn't home in Alabama, she called and checked on them at least once a day. While in Bama, my father would spend time with his brothers, sisters, and cousins. During that time, he would unwind and decompress from life back in Cleveland.

Later in life, I learned that being home was his escape. There was so much going on in his life that we had no idea about. So, trips back to Bama were always needed and wanted. Furthermore, Northport always boasted better weather, a relaxed vibe, and a loving atmosphere.

Let me tell you about my grandparents. My maternal grandmother was a favorite in Northport, mostly because she fed half the town. Mrs. Gussie Mae Jenkins was a cook by trade and worked as the cafeteria supervisor at Riverside High School for years, feeding thousands of local kids. She used those cooking skills every day at home. As far back as I can remember, she was retired from her job at the high school—but not her work within the house. She had a routine that never failed. Grandma would wake up early and cook breakfast around 8 a.m. She had one rule. She would always tell us, "Cook your own eggs." In her years of experience, Grandma knew people liked their eggs prepared differently. She didn't do all that because she needed to prepare dinner.

She would skip lunch and have dinner ready by 3 p.m. every day—not to mention it was a new dinner every night. We'd usually eat leftovers for lunch if we ate lunch. Grandma cooked everything from pot roast and greens to mac and cheese, yams, and black-eyed peas. Those were just some of my favorites. Occasionally, we would order out, mostly ribs from the local BBQ spot, but she always made the side dishes. The fridge and our bellies were always full at Grandma's. She was always three meals prepared and three steps ahead of us.

My maternal grandfather, who family and friends called "Bubba," was your classic Southern gentleman. His priorities were God, family, and work. He was a master plasterer—a highly skilled professional in the craft, science, and practice of plastering. He worked a lot with his hands. I remember feeling like my grandfather could build anything. I wasn't the only one; he won several awards through Northport, Tuscaloosa, and the state. As a master plasterer, he managed and supervised plastering crews, which allowed him to get to know many people throughout the city. But he wasn't social. He was a family man, and that mattered to him, a quality he passed down to my mother.

Whenever we drove to Alabama, we stayed at my mother's parents' house. Imagine a party of five, which included my parents, my two sisters, and me, squeezed into a three-bedroom, two-bathroom ranch-style house with no basement or attic. My parents always had a room, but my sisters and I had to rush to claim our spots for a good night's rest.

We visited every year, sometimes more than once a year. We never missed Thanksgiving at Grandma's. Sometimes we'd celebrate other holidays there too. It was the only time I'd see all my cousins, as my Aunt Sharron and her children would come from Indiana. My uncle, who we called "Brother," lived across the field from Grandma's house.

He and his kids were already over at Grandma's house each week, but it became an everyday thing when the family was in town. This was cool because Uncle Brother's children were around my age, so I had someone to hang out with. Not only did the family stop by, but my grandparents always had other visitors. We always heard the doorbell at least twice a day. While people said they came to pay respects to the

Jenkinses, I think they were just trying to get a plate. But no matter the reason or the season, everybody flocked to the Jenkins residence for good people, family fun, and great food.

Being the man my grandfather was, he made sure we didn't miss church, even when we visited. We started the day at 9 a.m. with Sunday school, staying until the church service wrapped up around 2 p.m. In Southern culture, church is often an all-day affair, and you must dress in your Sunday best. While I never looked forward to the all-day escapade, the part after church was always the best. On Sundays after church, we always went to Ryan's buffet. Ryan's is a buffet that serves the best chicken and rolls I've ever had! We ignored the fact that the chicken was deep-fried and the rolls were loaded with butter; it was our only restaurant meal when staying with my grandparents. So we ate up!

My father's parents both died young. That never stopped us from spending time with my father's siblings. We always visited my aunts, uncles, and cousins on the Prewitt side of the family. Hanging with the Prewitts was a different vibe than with the Jenkinses.

The Prewitts are your true Bama Proud Southerners: hardcore University of Alabama fans, proud to scream, "Roll Tide!" after every game. Hard workers with pure hearts who take care of business during the week and know how to unwind on weekends. My aunts and uncles loved my father. Aunt Dean once told my sister and me that our father reminded her of Denzel Washington because he was always cool. Daddy Cool was always the one to get the party started. To this day, my older cousins talk about how cool and great an uncle he was—an impression that always remains.

It was always Southern classics when we ate at the Prewitts'. Uncle Mike never hesitated to hop on the grill or host a classic fish fry. The seasoning was perfect every time. I loved those classics, but there was never a vegetable in sight. Interestingly, my aunt once told me she was first introduced to broccoli by my mother. In the South, the only veggies we ate were black-eyed peas, greens, and sweet potatoes.

Love and low stress characterized my parents' immediate environment, despite their upbringing in the stressful Jim Crow South. They ate lots of "soul food," but the crucial factor was that it was cooked at home. Eating out was for an occasion, not for convenience. They could control what went into their food—the amount of butter, salt, oils, and other hidden ingredients.

Of course, sometimes bad habits catch up with us. From the work he did, my grandfather developed environmental cancer, but thankfully, it went into remission. He also struggled with diabetes, but managed it well. My mother's sister also has diabetes, and my uncle is prediabetic, indicating a genetic tendency. My grandfather developed severe arthritis from years of working with his hands, and at one point, prostate cancer. Even with all that, he lived a long life—ninety-three years young, passing in 2018.

My grandmother always got rave reviews at doctor visits until she turned ninety. The only thing she battled was severe asthma. She was active, even into her early nineties—it would take an act of God to get Gussie Mae to sit down. Always trying to wash a dish, cook, clean, or tend to her flowers. Her activity helped minimize health issues.

One day, doing her usual routine, she slipped, fell, and broke her hip. That marked the start of her decline. A woman who looked seventy at ninety finally began to show her age. What we thought was stubbornness for not sitting down was her way of staying young. That's a valuable lesson in the importance of staying physically active. Just walking around the house can help extend your life and keep you feeling young. She never fully regained her mobility, which allowed issues like high blood pressure to set in. Eventually, she succumbed to dementia, passing in 2022 at ninety-six.

As I mentioned before, my father's parents passed away early, so I didn't spend much time with them. My paternal grandmother was a stay-at-home wife who cared for the house and kids, as Southern women often did. She died in 1980 at fifty-two from stomach cancer. My father was thirty. She passed away six years before I was born. From what I understand, my father took her death very hard; he was extremely close to her. Grandpa Prewitt was a truck driver, working for the city's sanitation department. I vaguely remember him—he passed when I was four, in 1990, at fifty-seven. My father was forty.

Even though cancer took both my Prewitt grandparents, that has never been an issue for my sisters or me; no high cholesterol has ever been reported by any of my Prewitt aunts and uncles. But this is where Mr. Morrow comes in. To be aware of any health risks, we have to look at him, since he is my dad's biological father. Not growing up with Mr. Morrow, my father was curious but never got the answers he wanted. Mr. Morrow and my father never had a true relationship—just the occasional public meetup. Mr. Morrow died in 1966 at forty-three. My father was only fifteen. Mr. Morrow had other children; my father was connected with some, not all.

Two of Mr. Morrow's sons ended up in Cleveland and started a business together—a significant turning point in our family's story. My uncles were one of my father's limited means for family health history. One uncle, unfortunately, drowned in a fishing accident. The other, Uncle Dennis, shared health struggles with my father—both had high cholesterol. Uncle Dennis smoked, developed other issues, and eventually underwent brain aneurysm surgery. There, doctors discovered that his arteries were thinner and weaker than usual, signaling an inherited genetic problem from Mr. Morrow. While the surgery succeeded, he later died of a heart attack at fifty-six, in 2006, two years after my father.

Knowing my family's health history prompted my doctors to test me for high cholesterol at a young age. That allowed me to know I was living with the condition. But what if I hadn't known or had no relationship with my dad? I would have had no way to discover potential future issues. Like my father, I might have found out too late. That's why, when you know better, you do better. Once you know, you can take action to keep your health in check. Screening tests can help catch rising risk factors like high cholesterol and high blood pressure, and can provide early detection for diseases like cancer. After the results, doctors can determine whether a condition is genetic and whether it can be managed through lifestyle changes. The earlier you test, the sooner you can catch something at its most treatable.

I encourage you to be curious about your family. You'll learn not only about health history but also amazing, inspiring, and heartbreaking stories. Even as I write this book, I continue to learn new things about my family that I never knew. Whether the stories make you laugh or cry, a story can be a lesson, a message, or a call to action. You might discover things that change your life. Those conversations could even save your life. But most of all, it gets you one step closer to being #HeartStrong.

3

"Cleveland Is the Reason"

Let's go back to 1972. It was before my time, but historically, it was a good time. *The Godfather* debuted in theaters nationwide, becoming the year's highest-grossing film. Richard Nixon was reelected, and the infamous Watergate scandal was just beginning. Al Green's "Let's Stay Together" climbed the Billboard charts and became a timeless classic. For my parents, life was moving at a mile a minute. They made many big decisions this year and had plenty to celebrate. In 1972, their lives changed forever, and "Cleveland is the reason."

Before Cleveland, my parents met back in elementary school in Northport. My dad said he saw my mother at Matthews Elementary School and knew then that she would be his wife. What seemed like a bold claim from a grade-schooler turned out to be true, even though my mother didn't feel the same way until high school. They dated around eleventh or twelfth grade. After high school, my parents left Northport for school.

My mother went to a business school in Atlanta. She was one of the top shorthand notetakers—a valuable skill. Using a system of abbreviations and symbols to represent words and phrases, shorthand note-taking allows for faster information recording compared to traditional longhand writing. Shorthand finds frequent use where quick information capture is crucial—for instance, during lectures or meetings. Her skills made her highly sought after. She was a top recruit in the field of executive assistants. Unsurprisingly, my mother has always been hardworking, determined, and creative.

My mother is a praying woman. She is also one of the most selfless people I know. While naturally shy, my mother has a caring, playful, and thoughtful spirit. While growing up, I saw her make sacrifices for people and her family to ensure they were okay. If she had five dollars, she would give a person $3.25. Sometimes, she wouldn't even get it back, but if she cared for you, it didn't matter. Unlike my father, just like her dad, she isn't a big people person but is a family person. She will do anything for you if you are worthy enough to be considered family. My mother has always been very private. Knowing my mother, she probably won't even want me saying this much about her. I may be telling too much! Even with so many opportunities waiting for her in Atlanta, she never wavered from the "Family's first" motto. My mother would frequently return to Alabama to be with her family. Upon completing school, my mother turned down offers to be an executive assistant to be with my father, starting a new family.

My father was the first in his family to go to college. He went north to Huntsville, Alabama, to attend Alabama A&M University. While at Alabama A&M, he pledged Kappa Alpha Psi Fraternity. As a kid, I knew little about Greek life. My father never discussed it with me. But I have many memories of him and his involvement in his fraternity. As a kid, I would see him embrace anyone sporting those funny-looking letters on their chests in red and white. He took me to several events and introduced me to all of his fraternity brothers. Still, none of it made sense to me. I didn't fully understand Greek life until I got to college. My dad and I share many similarities, and those similarities play a significant role in this story.

In the spring of '72, at twenty-one, my parents married. My father hadn't even graduated yet, as he was still a senior in college. However, shortly after, in June, he graduated from Alabama A&M with a degree in accounting. Later that summer, my parents moved to Cleveland. My father landed a job in accounting at ABC Accounting. He was already familiar with Cleveland, having spent summers with his aunt there during his high school years. But it was a new land for my mother; this was the first time she had been so far away from her family.

While my parents were far from their family, they started their own, beginning with my oldest sister. In January 1973, at twenty-two, my parents had their first child, Allegra, who we affectionately call Shena. Shena is thirteen years older than I am, so she practically raised me. My earliest memories of her date back to the early '90s, when she would visit home from college. Her style and vibe were reminiscent of characters from shows like *A Different World* and movies like *School Daze*. I always imagined that's what her college life was like. I saw her quite often. It seemed like my father made the three-hour trip to Springfield, Ohio, to pick her up every weekend.

After a few years, my parents settled in Cleveland, having learned to navigate a new city far from home with a toddler. In 1977, they bought a house in Warrensville Heights. My two sisters and I were raised there. Warrensville is a small suburb located near Cleveland, with a population of approximately ten thousand. When my parents moved into the neighborhood, it was predominantly an Italian neighborhood, but by the time I grew up there, it had become predominantly Black. Since Warrensville is located right on the border of Cleveland, it has always felt like it is part of the larger city. The only differences were the mayor, the school district, and taxes.

Not only did my parents buy a house that year, but they also welcomed my sister Jocelyn to the family in January. My sisters' birthdays are seven days apart, four years apart. They were extremely close. Jocelyn and I were also close. We spent most of our time together in childhood, despite being nine years apart. Before Shena went to college, Jocelyn and I shared a room. Whenever I had nightmares or couldn't sleep, Jocelyn would be right there to help. Like my mother, Jocelyn wasn't a people person but was a family person. While she was reserved, she wasn't shy. She was a fierce competitor.

Jocelyn was a three-sport athlete in high school. She lettered multiple years in volleyball, basketball, and track. She was the only one of us to attend a private high school, Hawken School. She was also the most well-traveled of the family. Jocelyn was the only one to go to an out-of-state school—in Iowa. Going to college in Iowa was a whole new world for a Cleveland girl. No family close by. We were 621 miles away, a nine-hour, thirty-minute drive, so no weekend visits home. Cornfields replaced corner stores. This was the '90s—no cell phones, no FaceTime, just expensive collect calls from dorm payphones. While it was challenging, she powered through undergrad and law school in Iowa, even meeting her future husband there.

I was born in 1986, the last of my siblings. By this time, my parents were thirty-five and had settled into their lives. I completed our party of five. By the time I was born, my parents had found their community. They found a church home that was very important to them. My father wanted to make sure that we put God in the middle of everything we did, so we never missed a Sunday at Trinity Methodist Church. It was a small church with a congregation of close to fifty people. All of the families knew each other. My sisters and I made some of our first friends at church. My parents also had close relationships with other members of the congregation. My father served as the church treasurer. He had a gift for numbers and used that gift to balance the church's financial books and records.

This is how I remember my childhood days in Warrensville. I inherited my compassion, creativity, and sense of family from my mother, while my father instilled in me his heart, pride, and the value of keeping my word. My sisters introduced me to culture and always had my back. We were a close-knit family. But eventually, things changed. Major events arose that transformed both me and my family, bringing heartbreaks, headaches, and more, all of which contributed to our story. Some experiences could be prevented, while others were unavoidable. The house in Warrensville was my parents' first and only home. There were opportunities to move, but we never took them. Throughout all the good and bad memories, there has always been—and always will be—a great deal of love in that house, which will forever remain my home.

4

Sauce on Everything

What if I told you that if you took a kielbasa, put it in a hot dog bun, and topped it off with French fries, coleslaw, and barbecue sauce, it would be one of the best things you've ever tasted? It's called a Polish Boy, not to be confused with a po'boy. A Polish Boy is native to Cleveland, and it's a Cleveland classic. It's so good that people drive from far distances just to get their hands on one. According to Esquire, an American men's magazine, Cleveland's Polish Boy received the accolade of being one of the best sandwiches in America. Even Iron Chef Michael Symon called the Polish Boy "the best thing I ever ate" on his Food Network show, *The Best Thing I Ever Ate,* where he featured Seti's version of the Cleveland staple.

Cleveland has some of the best food in the country, making it hard for my family to avoid some of the most popular dishes. Corned beef sandwiches, world-famous Polish Boys, and chicken and rib dinners were irresistible dishes that our family enjoyed quite a bit. Much of it reminded us of Southern cooking that we knew and loved. While it wasn't quite the same, it was enough to satisfy our cravings for Southern classics. Even today, my mouth waters over the thought of these foods, ignoring the amount of salt, butter, and cooking oils they use to make these creations. Again, while dining out is convenient and tasty, you do not know how the food is prepared. You take a gamble whenever you put your appetite in the hands of others.

Growing up, my mother had all of Grandma's recipes and got pretty good at recreating her best dishes. Mom didn't cook as much as Grandma did due to other obligations, but she managed to cook four days a week. Work took away much of my mother's attention, and my father would step in when that happened. Just as my mother picked up her cooking skills from her family, so did my dad. He was great on the grill but needed some work in other areas. Thankfully, my sister Shena eventually took over cooking duties; her skills were heaven-sent.

At one point, my mother explored recipes outside traditional Southern dishes, trying healthier options in an attempt to eat cleaner and leaner. For instance, we switched from ground beef to ground turkey. Ground turkey is usually leaner and therefore healthier than ground beef because it contains lower amounts of saturated fat and calories. We also incorporated more vegetables into our dinners. We increased foods like fish for the omega-3 benefits that can help lower LDL and triglyceride levels. I must admit that we didn't pay close attention to food labels and nutritional facts, especially when ordering from our local restaurants.

Which brings us back to the Cleveland classics. Foods like corned beef sandwiches are made with fresh corned beef on rye bread, topped with mustard, and accompanied by a pickle on the side. But my favorite was when we ordered from the local BBQ spots. There are so many to choose from in the city. Like my parents, many Black Southerners migrated to Cleveland, bringing their family recipes with them. We usually got rib slabs, tips, pork shoulder sandwiches, fried wing dinners, and those world-famous Polish Boys from these spots. As a Cleveland native, there is only one way to order these foods: by asking for

"Sauce on everything."

Sauce on everything is when BBQ sauce is poured all over your plate. The sauce drenches everything, from the meats to the French fries. As amazing as a pool of BBQ sauce is on our food, it is also high in almost everything terrible. Salt, sugar, butter—you name it, it's there, so it's always best to have these things in moderation. If sauce on everything is done daily, it could speed up any underlying health issues. After eating, my family would always ask, "Did you get enough?" and demand that we finish our plates. That was a Southern thing. It was about having a full belly and feeling satisfied. As much as I ate—with all the salt, butter, and fat—you would think I would have been huge.I was a skinny kid, but I was also very active.

Being an active kid helped me turn all that food into fuel as I played outside. I was always outside, from snow days to the hottest summer days. We didn't have social media, which was the best thing ever because it forced us to be outside and have fun. While some games were classic, others I would not recommend for today's youth.

We played games like Manhunt, a version of hide-and-seek with no base. It was our excuse to run all over the neighborhood. The funny thing is, no one knew how to end this game. You would get caught and turned into a hunter, or you would hide until people were tired of looking. Any Bounce was another classic in the neighborhood. It was our version of every-man-for-himself baseball. We would substitute a baseball for a bouncy tennis ball. If the batter got a hit, you had to catch the tennis ball on the first bounce. If you did, then it was your turn to bat. Chasing down tennis balls in the middle of the street was top-notch fun and a lot of running.

Every day felt like the street Olympics. Not only was our street already overpopulated with children of all ages, but kids from the surrounding streets would also come out to play. We'd cycle around until we spotted someone outdoors. On a good summer weekend day, we'd gather at least forty kids outside; on slower days, about twelve of us would meet up. We always had enough for five-on-five pickup basketball games with other teams waiting, and enough for seven-on-seven backyard or street football games. We had the numbers and crazy ideas, which led to some truly wild games.

As a child, one of my favorite reckless games was our version of street football. And when I say street, we played in the actual street. We had this thing we called Sideline Pop. On our street was the road, a small patch of grass, the sidewalk, and the start of someone's front lawn. When we played Sideline Pop, it was tag on the street, but if you went into the grass area before the sidewalk and front yard of a house, you could get tackled in that grassy area. Yes, there were many premature tackles, where people would get tackled on the curb or slide over to the sidewalk and get scraped up. It made us who we were, which was roughhouse kids.

As dangerous as all this sounds, we avoided major injuries and trouble because there were always eyes on us. Our street was a true village. Every parent in the neighborhood raised us. We became their kids, and they became our instant parents when anyone got hurt or did something wrong.

When I wasn't outside in the neighborhood, I participated in different programs and camps, such as basketball camp, summer league baseball, and a sports camp at our local community college. Camp would start at 8 a.m. and last until about 3 or 4 p.m. After returning home from camp, I would go outside to play with friends. I would never sit down, according to my mother. While I loved my friends and always looked forward to the summer, I spent many of those summers in Northport. Those were unforgettable moments with my cousins. Being the same age, we used to play outside a lot when we were younger. I even remember participating in a sports camp there for a few summers.

I'm getting lost down memory lane, but there is a point. Being active at an early age laid the foundation that would ultimately save my life later on. Physical health is crucial for kids. The CDC recommends that children aged six through seventeen engage in at least sixty minutes of moderate to vigorous physical activity daily. As you can see from my childhood, or "back in my day," we had no problem reaching that recommendation. Being outside so much, we improved our social skills by learning how to deal with issues and handle conflicts. We learned to apologize, forgive, and sometimes forget if there was a fight. We were developing strong bones and muscles, improving our cardiovascular fitness, and battling childhood obesity by controlling our weight—even after a meal with wings, slaw, fries, and sauce on everything.

Times are different from when I was growing up. I would go to the basketball court to find friends, but now, kids are going to the basketball court through their gaming systems to see who else is online. Traditional outdoor play, such as running, jumping, and playing tag, has been replaced in many cases by more sedentary activities. Kids are now captivated by their screens and have no interest in being outdoors. But as the saying goes, "It's best to start them early." Creating the early foundation of active movement made it easier to maintain as an adult. It allowed me to develop a competitive side that motivates and pushes me to this day. Remember, being #HeartStrong isn't just for adults but for kids too. And the earlier the commitment starts, the better the chances of living a longer, healthier life.

5

"Do You Know How Many Calories Are in That?!"

My First Warning

I had just announced to my teacher—and my whole class—that I suffered from high cholesterol. Her initial response was shock and disbelief, followed by rapid-fire questions about my eating habits and calorie intake. "What's a calorie?" she quizzed me. I had never heard of calories in my life. Feeling pressured to answer, I simply said, "I don't know." I felt like I was in trouble. This became a teachable moment for the class and an unforgettable lesson for me.

Let's take one more trip to 1999, to Mrs. Dunning's home economics class at Warrensville Heights Middle School. Mrs. Dunning was always cool. She was the type of teacher you didn't cross because if you behaved, she would treat you well, but if you acted out, she would get you in line quickly. I also loved home economics class because we got to eat! The class covered everything related to the house, including cooking, knitting, and other skills that would be useful. It was always cool to me when we cooked in class! And we got to eat what the class cooked. I loved that we did this as a class, because I wasn't good at cooking.

Since food was a subject of this class, the topic of cholesterol came up. Certain foods contain cholesterol, and too much LDL cholesterol can lead to health issues.

"I have high cholesterol," I said calmly and casually. It wasn't a big deal to me, but it was for Mrs. Dunning. "What?!" was her immediate response, as she was utterly shocked. From her perspective, I was way too young to have high cholesterol, and she was right. Looking back, I get why Mrs. Dunning had the reaction she did. Usually, cholesterol is controllable. It catches up to people after years of poor eating habits, lack of exercise, and other factors. But that wasn't quite the case for me, and as active as I was, exercise wasn't enough to keep my cholesterol levels in check.

So, let's talk more about my genetics. The medical term for my condition is familial hypercholesterolemia, or FH for short. Most people can manage their cholesterol levels through lifestyle and habit changes. For me, it's caused by genetics, so even changing my lifestyle wouldn't be enough to live with this condition. According to Yale Medicine, FH is one of the more common genetic disorders in the U.S., affecting about one in 250 people. FH is what's known as an autosomal dominant disorder, so a child has a 50 percent chance of inheriting a mutated gene from a parent who has the mutation.

Cholesterol isn't a bad thing. Your body needs it to function correctly. Cholesterol helps your body make cell membranes, certain hormones, and vitamin D; it also produces compounds that aid in fat digestion. The cholesterol in your blood comes from two sources: the foods you eat—like egg yolks, meat, poultry, fish, and dairy products—and your liver. Your liver makes all the cholesterol your body needs. A normal liver has a receptor protein that tells the body to stop producing cholesterol.

Unfortunately, in my family, some of us were born with a genetic mutation that does not tell our bodies to stop producing cholesterol, which leads to abnormally high LDL cholesterol levels. The cholesterol and other fats carried in your bloodstream are called lipoproteins. The two most commonly known lipoproteins are low-density lipoproteins (LDLs) and high-density lipoproteins (HDLs). During cholesterol screenings, these are the two primary things they check for, along with triglycerides, which are a type of fat in your blood that your body uses for energy.

We consider HDL the "good cholesterol" because it absorbs cholesterol from other parts of the body and carries it back to the liver, where it is then removed. High levels of HDL can lower the risk of heart disease and stroke. Experts classify LDL as the "bad" cholesterol. LDL cholesterol can contribute to the formation of plaque buildup in the arteries, a condition known as atherosclerosis. Atherosclerosis narrows arteries, blocking blood flow to the heart and other organs and ultimately leading to heart disease and stroke.

HDL is the one number you want to be high, ideally above 60 mg/dL. Your LDL "bad" cholesterol should be below 100 mg/dL. Overall, your total cholesterol should be below 200 mg/dL. From there, 200–239 mg/dL is borderline high, and anything above 240 mg/dL is high. For teenagers, those numbers are even lower: The ideal recommendation is less than 170 mg/dL, with LDL levels below 100 mg/dL, which is similar to the recommendation for adults. However, the HDL level is recommended to be 45 mg/dL or higher, compared to the 60 mg/dL recommended for adults.

At fourteen years old, my total cholesterol level was around 300.

But I wasn't the only one in the family with this condition. Shena also suffered from FH. She first discovered this at the age of twenty-two. She recalls being 120 pounds, a size 2, with a dangerously high cholesterol level. She, too, was told at an early age that she might not live to be thirty years old. Sound familiar? Thankfully, she has.

When it came to my cholesterol, fortunately, my HDL number was high, but it drove my overall number up, and I was still at risk of a heart attack or stroke. FH can also cause other health problems related to excess cholesterol buildup in tissues other than the heart and blood vessels. If cholesterol accumulates in the tissues that attach muscles to bones (tendons), it causes characteristic growths called tendon xanthomas. These growths most often affect the Achilles tendons, which attach the calf muscles to the heels, and tendons in the hands and fingers. Yellowish cholesterol deposits known as xanthelasmas can develop under the skin of the eyelids. Cholesterol can also accumulate at the edges of the eye's clear front surface (the cornea), leading to a gray- or blue-colored ring called arcus cornealis.

If these signs are caught early enough, your doctor will start you on multiple cholesterol-lowering medications, such as statins, to help control your cholesterol levels. But my mother declined this because she felt I was way too young to start medicines I would be on for the rest of my life. We had already seen my dad battle through his issues, and my mother didn't want the same for me. While physical activity is essential and encouraged after diagnosis, it is usually not enough to lower your cholesterol to a healthy level on its own.

Back to Mrs. Dunning's class. Now, the conversation had become more of a thing than I wanted it to. "What do you eat for lunch?" she asked with such pure concern in her voice. But I didn't want to tell her because I knew I wasn't doing myself any favors with my school lunch selections. Middle school was the first time we could buy school lunches. Before that, back in sixth grade and earlier, we would bring our lunches to school, so our parents controlled what we ate.

You can imagine what it's like when you give a thirteen-year-old the option of what to eat. Here's a hint: It wasn't vegetables. The only lunch foods I looked forward to were pizza, burgers, and chicken tenders. When it wasn't one of those days, I would usually save my two dollars and skip lunch. Instead, I would hit the vending machine for a Little Debbie Honey Bun and a Lay's Classic Potato Chips bag. After using the vending machine, I would usually have money left over, which I would use at the corner store on the way home, leading me to buy more chips. These were the days of four chip bags for a dollar, so there were a lot of chips. Upon hearing about my food choices, Mrs. Dunning was still stunned and processing this information.

"Do you know how many calories are in that?"

I did not understand what a calorie was, but I had to answer because she had asked a question. Mrs. Dunning already knew that I didn't know. "Go downstairs and buy yourself a honey bun and a bag of chips out of the vending machine, and let's see," she said. Our school wasn't big. It was only two levels. It took about five minutes to go to the cafeteria vending machine and come back. Right then, Mrs. Dunning wasted no time flipping each item over to read the food labels.

"There are 240 calories in Lay's Classic Potato Chips," Mrs. Dunning said. And when she said it, she made sure the entire class heard. *"There are 360 calories in a Little Debbie Honey Bun!"* That one felt even louder than the first announcement. From calories to cholesterol and all the other food facts, Mrs. Dunning continued to read each point out loud.

She highlighted ingredients that were the most harmful and certainly contributing to my health issues.

I will never forget the moment Mrs. Dunning called me out in class. While it was embarrassing at the time, it has become one of the most valuable lessons I've learned in life. It was the first time anybody had pointed out the food label to me. Often overlooked, food labels can help you make informed decisions on what you are eating and how much you should eat of it. Many things would have been different if I had only made this a habit. I am not saying I wouldn't have had a heart attack, but paying attention to food labels would have helped me manage my outcomes better. That day with Mrs. Dunning was also an early indicator of the trouble I could face, which is why I still do two things to this day: One is staying away from honey buns. Since that day, I have never had a honey bun again. The second is always to read the food labels. These days, I pay close attention to serving sizes, sodium, and ingredients—and to avoid getting caught slipping again, I always check the calories.

6

Daddy Cool

Many days, my father would take me on his ride around the city as he handled his business. I was too young to ask questions; I just enjoyed the time spent together and the opportunity to see more of the town outside Warrensville. One day we stopped at this bar. I don't remember much about the location, but I do remember it was on the corner in a residential neighborhood. I knew he wasn't going to drink; he was going to find someone to have a chat about some business between them.

In my father's line of work, he dealt with many blue-collar workers who used their hands or had a specific trade. Most of these guys had habits such as alcohol, gambling, women, and even drug problems. It was common for my father to be in some of the most dangerous places to find his workers and even save them from harmful, sometimes life-threatening situations. So, when it came to this guy, my father needed to see him that day. He knew he could find him at that bar, as he would usually stop for his midday happy hour.

"Stay here, and I'll be right back." It was typical for him to leave me in the car while he handled his business. I never overthought it, as I usually found ways to entertain myself. I never timed how long he was gone; I always sat and waited patiently. But this day, suddenly I saw my father storming out of the bar, followed by a group of guys. He wasn't running, but he had a brisk pace, like he was walking away from a confrontation. It looked like something out of a movie as many men and young kids walked after him. Some even still had their pool sticks in their hands. My father got back in the car, and he was angry. Something happened in that bar, and because of the energy and the men chasing him, it couldn't have been anything good. "I don't want to do this in front of your son," one man said, but that didn't bother my father. He responded with some pretty strong words back and then sped off.

I have always remembered that incident and how my father showed no fear. He would have tried to take on all of them if I hadn't been there. I always heard stories about my father from my family and his fraternity brothers. My father wasn't afraid of anything or anyone. When people talk about him, everyone always mentions how fierce he was, yet he could still make new friends and leave a lasting impression wherever he went. Since I only have seventeen years of memories with my father, hearing stories about him helps me paint a picture and learn who he was and what people thought of him.

Writing this book taught me more about why they said those things in stories about him. I had to research to ensure that my stories and history were as accurate as possible, which allowed me to learn a lot about my father. I will admit it has been quite therapeutic for me. I would always hear family close to my dad tell me, "Man, you're just like your daddy," from our personalities and our mannerisms to the way we phrase certain things, even down to the walk we share. Most say I am a mirror image of my father.

Until recently, I never knew what that meant since his life ended so soon. People have different personas, and I only got to know one of those for my father: "Dad." I didn't know who he was except my dad. When you lose a parent before adulthood, you miss out on critical conversations in life. For me, some things have felt incomplete. I've had burning questions that I would have liked to ask my father but never got the chance to. From a life perspective, I would have loved to hear his advice on family, love, and growing up and becoming my own man.

From the time we spent together when he was alive, I remember him as a very active man. He ran several marathons, played racquetball regularly, and, like me, loved biking. He introduced me to biking when I was young. Maybe that's why I love it so much now. One of my favorite memories of my dad is riding our bikes together through the parks around the city. We had many adventures on our bikes, and it was our quality time together. While my dad was active, we didn't play or compete against each other. There was no playing one-on-one basketball or footracing, because he was "old." It's funny I say *old*, as I am now around the same age as when my parents had me. With such an age gap, Sam Edward wasn't chasing me around the house.

As impressive as he was, he had his vices, as everyone does. He developed some bad habits in his search for a connection with the Morrow side of the family. That unfulfilled need for acceptance controlled his life more than he would admit. But my mother saw it all in real time, even things that he could not see. Some vices he picked up were short-lived, and some were long-term. At one point, he picked up a smoking habit, but that was one of the short-lived habits. He stopped smoking before I was born, but my uncles continued to be heavy smokers. Drinking alcohol was one of those habits that stuck with him.

My father wasn't a heavy drinker during the week or at home. Sometimes, he would come home after too many, and my mom would confront him, but it wasn't a toxic habit. One thing my father did faithfully was to have a nightly beer. He didn't get drunk; it was more to unwind after a long day. Like most families in the '90s, our family huddled around the TV to catch the usual nightly TV lineups. If we weren't watching our favorite shows, we would watch sports, especially if a Cleveland team was playing. My father was a huge Cleveland fan.

Our family spent time bonding around the TV in the attic of our house, which we fondly called "the third floor." It was a renovated attic with carpet, family pictures, his working desk, a lounging chair, and the family couch. My mother had her spot on the couch, and my sisters and I contended for the last spot. We had to sit on the carpet if we didn't win a place on the couch. Whenever my father wanted a beer, it was up to my sisters and me to go down to the first floor, where the kitchen was located, to get him a cold one from the refrigerator. I miss those simple yet cherished moments that brought us closer as a family. This is how we bonded and spent our time together.

My dad was brilliant and one of the best in his career field. My father was a cost engineer—a multidisciplinary professional who manages projects and their resources throughout those projects' life cycles. That includes managing project cost—estimating, cost control, cost forecasting, and investment appraisal—and risk analysis. Cost engineers budget, plan, and monitor investment projects.

From what I've been told, he was a wizard at this, and some of the biggest companies nationwide sought him out. There was a company in Philadelphia that offered my father the opportunity to work for them. They offered an excellent salary; help with relocation, including a new house for the family; and employment for my mother. Yet, he declined.

My father knew who he wanted to work for, and it made him proud. It wasn't arrogance. Growing up in the South, he saw firsthand how the system left Black folks behind. That experience drove him to apply his skills where they mattered most—helping the people he could relate to.

He knew his worth and was confident in his abilities. However, he waived all that to grow closer to his brothers. Eventually, he and his brothers on the Morrow side started Progressive Brothers Construction Incorporated. We dropped the C and shortened it to PBI. During my lifetime, my father mainly worked for PBI, which was the setting for a lot of the significant events within our family, including his first major health event.

It was the summer of 1994, and my sister Shena was home from college. She occasionally worked at the PBI office during her summer break to earn money. She answered the phone at the office, filed paperwork, and performed other secretarial duties. Since it was our dad's office, she thought it was optional—until my mother reminded her that she had no money and that working was the only way to earn it. That summer in '94, we were all happy she was in the office with him that day.

The PBI office was small. Usually, there were about three to five people in the office. But that day, my father and sister were the only ones there. My sister recalls that Dad wasn't looking or feeling great that day. He was pouring with sweat and looked fatigued. My father was a dark-skinned man, but still had a visibly purplish complexion. "I'll be right back. I'm going to the store," he yelled as he walked out the door. The store was within walking distance, so he was gone for about ten minutes. He bought a bottle of Mylanta, a medicine that relieves heartburn. "He chugged the Mylanta straight from the bottle," my sister recalls. It surprised her that he disregarded any of the suggested dosing recommendations. Even after drinking the entire bottle, he felt no relief.

"Do you want me to take you to the hospital?"

"Yes," my father answered quickly. He wasn't feeling any better. They hopped in the car for a quick trip. The hospital was only a short distance away from the office. When they arrived, they checked into the emergency room and assumed they would have to wait to be seen. Since my sister parked in the emergency lane, she had to find a parking space. She found a parking space quickly, but it wasn't quick enough. Dad was nowhere to be found when she returned to the emergency room. A doctor came out shortly to greet her. After he confirmed she was family, he delivered some devastating news.

"Your father just had a heart attack."

This was the first heart attack my father suffered from. This was also when he discovered he had high cholesterol. Since the number was so high, the doctors determined it was familial hypercholesterolemia. One might wonder, *Shouldn't a routine doctor's visit have revealed this?* Surprisingly, the answer is not necessarily. FH is often misdiagnosed. Doctors may not order cholesterol tests for young patients unless they have severe symptoms, such as a heart attack or stroke.

After all these years, my father learned for the first time that he was living with this genetic condition that could kill him. This brings us back to the significance of understanding your family's health history and any relevant issues. If he had known, he could have started treatment earlier and changed his lifestyle and habits. Who knows? He could still be here today. But the questions that went unanswered by the Morrow side of the family didn't give my father the chance to prepare. Even more ironic, at the time of his first heart attack, my father was the same age Mr. Morrow was when he passed away. Mr. Morrow died at forty-four years old, and my father was just a couple of months away from his forty-fourth birthday. But thankfully, it wasn't my father's day to die.

My father underwent open-heart double-bypass surgery. Bypass surgery is a procedure that improves blood flow to the heart by creating a detour around blocked or narrowed coronary arteries. That involved the doctors making a long incision down his chest and cracking his rib cage open to get to his heart so they could rework his arteries. He stayed in the hospital for just over a week, and being the man he was, he won the hearts of all the nurses caring for him.

When he left the hospital, all the nurses signed his heart-shaped pillow. I remember thinking how cool that pillow was. It was the first time I can remember seeing a pillow in a unique shape. And since I was so young, it reminded me of a cartoon character. When he returned home from the heart attack, he was different. He was healing from this traumatic experience, which changed his demeanor. He was getting used to his new "zipper" scar on his chest from surgery. But it wasn't the scar that was the issue—it was healing from having his breastbone cracked open. That healing time is typically six to eight weeks, so he was down for a bit, but once he recovered, he returned to work and his physical activities.

My father's heart attack was the reason my mother got more serious about her cooking and our eating habits, leading my mother to introduce broccoli to my father's side of the family. It was something new for everybody. My mother was determined to make switches to ensure we all ate better. She broke away from the traditional Southern cooking she was used to and learned new recipes lower in salt, fat, and harmful substances to hopefully ensure we never had to go through that again. Keep in mind that not only did Dad suffer from a heart attack due to high cholesterol, but my sister learned shortly after that she was living with this condition as well. While eating habits and lack of exercise are common causes of heart attacks and strokes, one factor that is commonly overlooked is stress. Genetics caused the first health event, but stress became the most significant cause of my dad's declining health.

Speaking of stress, let's revisit the bar situation my father was in. I found out what the bar beef was all about the day after the confrontation. My father had gone to the bar to find the man who had been contracted to work on our house. He hadn't been showing up, and my father had to track him down. The guy showed up the next day, and you could tell he was walking on eggshells with my dad. While things were still tense, my father softened his tone a bit but remained very direct. My dad won that battle. And the guy learned the hard way that you couldn't play my father. Disrespect from anyone would not be tolerated. His actions and how he handled that situation are lessons that have stuck with me. That was the most memorable moment for me, seeing my father as a boss. He showed no fear and ensured the man completed the work, with a discount for the trouble he put my father through.

But after the heart attack, my dad had to start being mindful of certain things and situations. Situations like that are stressful; stress is the last thing a heart attack survivor needs. But little did we know he was already in the middle of daily stressful situations—situations that were doing more harm than any bar fight would have done. Healing from a heart attack, along with all the other things that were going on in his life, it's best to describe this chapter in his life as stress, mess, and regrets.

7

Stress, Mess, and Regrets

Three years after my father's heart attack, he was back to his routine—with some adjustments, of course. My father was back to biking, running, and racquetball. He was back at work, using his gift for numbers to win bids on construction contracts for his company. The heart attack had been a wake-up call, making him aware of his genetic disease and reinforcing that it was manageable with a proper diet and medication. Per usual, he was back to being Superman. He was doing well—or so we thought. That changed on a weeknight in the fall of 1997.

My father had cousins in Cleveland from Alabama. While he had many friends, family was always his first choice for a night out, even if that meant just going out for a beer or two. But on this night, something felt different; he felt it as soon as he arrived home. Dad noticed he wasn't feeling well, but he tried to push through and continued with his nightly routine, getting ready for bed. Having settled down for the night, he noticed he still hadn't shaken the feeling. In 1997, the internet wasn't mainstream—only about 2 percent of the world was online—so he couldn't do an online search for his symptoms. Still, he knew what was happening. He turned to my mother while they were in bed and said in a very calm voice, "I think I am having a stroke."

For my father to admit something like that out loud was a breakthrough. As brilliant as he was, he was just as stubborn, especially when it came to medical care. He didn't trust doctors. He was the kind of person who would try an old-school home remedy before calling to make a doctor's appointment. Even during his first heart attack, if it hadn't been for my sister seeing the distress on his face and offering to take him to the hospital, he probably wouldn't have gone. Deferring and delaying treatment during significant chest pain is what the nurses and my cardiac rehab crew referred to as "cooking your heart," a figurative way to describe the intense physical and emotional trauma the heart experiences when you stall seeking medical treatment. It emphasizes the severity and damaging nature of the event—and it's preventable. The longer you wait, the more irreversible the heart damage. That's another reason it was a godsend that my sister was in the office the day of Dad's first heart attack.

The root of my father's distrust came from his experience growing up in Alabama. From cruel medical experiments on enslaved Black people to the Tuskegee syphilis experiment, there are many reasons for mistrust of the health care system that was—and still is—a major issue among Black people. According to CommonwealthFund.org, seven out of ten Black Americans say the health care system mistreats people like them, and 55 percent say they distrust it. That mistrust prevents people from getting the care they need—and this attitude is often passed down from generation to generation. But help isn't just needed for your body; it's also important for mental issues. While the world now understands and accepts that mental health issues are real, back in the late nineties when my dad got sick, serious stigmas prevented many from seeking the help they needed.

Maintaining mental health includes managing stress levels. Stress can lead to severe mental issues that alter the mind and the way it operates. For instance, stressful thinking can cause short-sightedness—focusing on immediate solutions rather than long-term consequences. Stressful thinking forces you to make more emotional decisions based on incomplete information.

While growing up, I remember that common statements and excuses for certain behaviors of troubled family members were things like, "Y'all know he's touched" or "He's not all there." Instead of asking questions to see if anything could be done to help, elder family members usually discouraged this, feeling there was nothing to do but stay away from them. Most families would turn a blind eye to mental health issues rather than intervene to help or prevent a downfall. Most families had that one person who was once a shining star but began drowning their problems in a bottle. But even when families noticed someone was, as we called it, "going through some things," no one suggested therapy. When I was growing up, therapy was considered to be for wealthy people, court-mandated treatment, or for the truly insane.

In reality, stress and unresolved mental health issues take a massive toll on your body. According to Gallup's 2024 data, 37% of adults worldwide felt stressed "a lot" the previous day—levels far above a decade ago. In the U.S., 51% of working women report frequent daily stress (vs. 39% of men). For the average person, stress is unlikely to cause sudden death, but if left unmanaged or untreated for a long time—especially with preexisting health conditions—stress can kill.

This brings us back to my father. We had no idea how much stress he was under because he normalized it, and so did we. He had a habit of working to distract himself from any problems, which explains why he rushed to return to normal activities so quickly. While work can temporarily distract from stress and provide a sense of control, relying on it as the primary way to cope is generally unsustainable and can have a negative impact on overall well-being. What's worse is that we later discovered working at PBI was a major source of stress in his life.

As I mentioned earlier, my father cofounded PBI with two brothers on the Morrow side of the family: Uncle David and Uncle Dennis. Uncle David was the oldest by three years, and my uncle Dennis and my father were the same age. This caused some tension—there was serious sibling rivalry. Uncle Dennis seized every opportunity to remind my father who the "true Morrow" was, but my dad still didn't know what a "real Morrow" was. He didn't have an ideal relationship with his own father, but he hoped to win over his siblings with his personality. That striving for acceptance caused him a tremendous amount of stress, which was the last thing he needed while dealing with his health issues.

According to AMR Therapy, the stress of not being accepted by family can have many adverse effects on a person's mental and physical health, including self-esteem issues, anxiety, depression, and more. Luckily, my dad didn't lack confidence, nor did he suffer from depression or anxiety, but he struggled with identity. All his life, he had to put together the pieces of what it meant to be a Morrow while also trying to set the standard for a Prewitt man.

So, the stress of acceptance and self-discovery most likely sped up my father's first heart attack. By that time, he had already been at PBI for many years and had gone through many difficulties. The Prewitts—who loved and adored him—were still in Alabama, which is why he was eager to return home on the weekends. Back in Cleveland, things got so bad that he faced serious legal issues related to PBI. He tackled these preventable issues directly to protect his brothers and the business, but that only landed him in more trouble—even jail time.

But to him, it was nothing, because he wanted to prove he was down for family. That drive for acceptance led my father down a dark path, ultimately compromising his decision-making abilities. Stressful thinking—even for someone as bright as my father—led him into situations he might not have otherwise entered. This mindset even led him to take charge of his own heart treatment, sometimes straying from doctors' orders, which only led to more health complications. The decisions he started making became increasingly impulsive, executed quickly with little time thinking them through. Decisions happen fast, and if you choose wrong, it can change your life—and those of the people around you, creating a ripple effect.

Back to that weeknight in 1997 when my father thought he was having a stroke. A stroke is different from a heart attack, but they are closely related. A stroke happens when part of the brain doesn't get the blood and nutrients it needs. Symptoms depend on which part of the brain is affected. Typically, part of the face or body may feel weak. Sometimes, a stroke affects speech or vision.

"What?" my mother said in disbelief. To her, he looked the same—nothing was visibly wrong. "Do you want to go to the hospital?" she asked. Once again, my father knew something wasn't right and accepted her offer. Usually, with a stroke, the American Heart Association teaches people to think "F.A.S.T."—an acronym that helps people recognize the signs and symptoms: *F* for face drooping (Does one side of the face droop, or is it numb?), *A* for arm weakness (Is one arm weak or numb?), *S* for speech difficulty (Is speech slurred?), and *T* for time to call 911 (A stroke is an emergency, and every minute counts. Call 911 immediately. Note the time when any symptoms first appear.). My mother had to help him out of bed as things worsened; she even called me in to assist. As she recalls, I was on one side, and she was on the other as we helped my father down the steps and into the car to go to the hospital late in the evening.

The hospital was just a two-minute drive away, saving precious time as we got him to the emergency room. After the medical staff checked him out, they confirmed his fear: He had indeed suffered a stroke—a silent stroke. Silent strokes can go unnoticed if the damaged area is small or located in a part of the brain that doesn't control vital functions. They can cause permanent brain damage and increase the risk of future strokes and dementia. They often have no symptoms, or the symptoms are not obvious or don't last long, but they are still harmful and can be fatal.

So here we go again. Just three years after my father's first heart attack, we were dealing with another major medical event. He was only forty-seven—not even fifty years old—and a man so active and fit. Why did these things keep happening to him? This time, his demeanor was different. During the heart attack, he had been a fighter, determined to get back on his feet. But with this stroke, he was distraught and emotional—sometimes saying things to the family that made little sense. I had never seen him like this before; I believe it was the first time I ever saw my father break down and cry. Seeing him like that, I thought he might not make it. That feeling spread throughout the family, making us all emotional. But it wasn't just the stroke—it was all the things he was dealing with that we didn't know about at the time, taking a physical toll on his health and body.

The stroke did damage in a lot of ways, both physically and emotionally. My father lost sight in one of his eyes and had to wear an eye patch, which impacted his ability to work and drive. He applied for disability, but his application was denied. I remember joking with him and playfully calling him a pirate to lighten the mood—he'd smile and tell me, "Shut up," but I could tell he appreciated the humor. He embraced the patch and made the best of it, learning how to manage with one eye. We weren't sure if he'd ever regain his eyesight, but after a few months, it fully returned.

After the stroke, his trips to the doctor and the amount of medicine he took both increased. My father had to carry a small bag with him at all times with various medicines and health-related items. He had to take his pills at specific times every day—a missed dose could be fatal. While these medicines kept him alive, they also made his daily life more difficult, causing internal issues like ulcers, easy bruising, and thin, watery blood.

I vividly remember how those medications changed things for him. One day, my father and I were out running errands and stopped at the hardware store. Since he worked in construction, he sometimes made store runs for his work crew if they couldn't leave the site. Some items are packaged in hard plastic that's nearly impossible to open without a knife. My father always carried a small Swiss Army knife for times like this. As usual, he carefully pulled up the blade to cut open the package—but this time, he accidentally cut himself. It was a simple cut, like a paper cut or a small gash on the finger. For most people, a minor cut like that is annoying but not serious—the bleeding usually stops in about five minutes. But not for him.

When my father cut his finger, it bled a lot—more than a healthy person's would. I never knew exactly what medicines he was taking, only that they were keeping him alive. That day, I realized what a blood thinner does. As he tended to the cut, the bleeding didn't stop easily. It felt like a scene from a horror movie—the blood was watery and just wouldn't stop. I'd never seen blood so thin and runny before. My father actually freaked out a bit, worried the cut wouldn't stop bleeding. He picked up his phone as if he needed to call for help, but then thought better of it. He went through several napkins trying to stop the bleeding. After about fifteen minutes, it finally stopped, but the aftermath was dramatic. If anyone had seen it, they might have thought he'd almost cut off his finger—that was the reality of life on those medications.

Experiences like this made my father realize he was human, not Superman. Early death became a realistic possibility for him, and he began picturing a world without himself. To prepare, he began estate planning, ensuring our family would be comfortable and secure in the event of his passing. He guided my mother through their finances, which included knowing which accounts were which, where to find important documents, and other practical information. For extra security, he even opened an emergency savings account for us

But as my father started to recover more fully, he also began researching alternative medicines. He read about how the American health system keeps people medicated rather than finding actual cures, and how different treatments can naturally lower cholesterol. With this research, he started to wean himself off the medicines prescribed by his doctor. Now, you might wonder: *Why would someone who'd already suffered a heart attack and a stroke consider doing this?* It goes back to the deep-rooted distrust many Black people have for doctors—an attitude I heard summed up often as a child: "The money isn't in the cure; it's the comeback." Along with trying alternative treatments, he became active again, both physically and socially. He picked up more hours at work—more than usual—and started going to more fraternity meetings; sometimes it felt like he had a meeting every week. My father was a popular guy, so this wasn't questioned. Even after a heart attack, open-heart surgery, and a stroke, he kept going—until those experimental changes caused a turn for the worse.

It was the fall of 1998. My mother worked as a leasing consultant at an apartment complex and had to work on weekends. Before she left for work one morning, she saw that my father wasn't feeling well.

"Do you want me to take you to the hospital?" she asked, concerned, but my father declined, thinking whatever was happening would pass. My mother went about her morning routine, got dressed, and headed downstairs, timing it perfectly, as she always did. As she was about to head out the door, she found my father lying on the ground in distress. This time, he admitted he needed to go to the hospital. My mother took him in, and once he was checked in, the doctors knew immediately what had happened.

"Ma'am, your husband just suffered a heart attack... again."

This time, there was no bypass surgery—instead, he had to get a stent placed. Once again, he'd developed dangerous blockages in his arteries from plaque buildup. My father's alternative medicine experiments hadn't helped—they'd made things worse. To me, this disproved the idea that doctors are only interested in keeping people medicated and never cured. It's never wise to stop heart treatment without consulting a doctor first. Remember: Doctors take an oath to save lives. Finding the right doctor—one you trust—means you can work together to create a treatment plan that works for you and your health.

As a family, we were confused. Why did this keep happening? We felt lost. As a child, I didn't realize how much this added to my own fears. My father was my role model—the blueprint for my life as I grew up. Not to mention, I'd already been diagnosed with high cholesterol around this time, so I started to quietly accept that this would happen to me, too. I was accepting a generational curse without even realizing it. While our genes were the same, our struggles and stresses were different. The stress that had built up and piled onto him was starting to affect his health in ways I didn't fully understand until later.

Again, stress doesn't kill you immediately, but it will catch up to you eventually. When you're stressed, your body releases hormones that increase your blood pressure and make your heart beat faster. This can lead to heart attacks, strokes, and more. When people are stressed, they sometimes turn to vices to cope—recreational drugs, alcohol, gambling, and other risky behaviors—which may only increase their chances of developing heart disease.

My father honestly thought he was going to die. This was his third major medical event and second heart attack in four years. Not to mention, he was between the ages his own parents had been when they passed away, so for him, this felt like living on borrowed time. Facing the possibility of death, most people start to reflect honestly on their lives—sometimes confessing things, seeking peace, or asking for forgiveness—because the consequences of those confessions seem less important when life itself is on the line.

One day in the hospital, my dad reflected on his life and unloaded a lot on my sister Jocelyn. She learned many things about him in that conversation. He went into detail about his life, things he'd done and what he'd had to do, and about our family—things we'd never known before. He told her how some of his actions and decisions had led to the health issues he was now facing. Sam Edward did not die that day, but a piece of our family did.

In the days that followed, Jocelyn wasn't the same. Her mood and energy changed, and she couldn't hide it. My mother, who always had a sixth sense about her children, picked up on it and asked why she was so down. We could never hide anything from her. Jocelyn couldn't hold in the information she'd been given, so she started sharing some details with my mom. After she heard everything and started to put it all together, my mother realized it was all one big mess.

A mess that needed time—apart—to be sorted out. As a kid, I didn't have all the details. All I knew was that it was a time of pain and regret. I hate that I never got the chance as an adult to hear Dad's side of the story or to know exactly what he told Jocelyn. All I know is that it threatened and tested our family to the point that my mother asked my father to leave the house. She had a lot of emotional unpacking and processing to do, and we all needed to figure out how to move forward—whether as a family or as individuals.

Things were also changing in my father's career. PBI was nearing its end; it had started to develop a bad reputation, which hurt its business. My father began to step back as he focused on addressing his health and family issues. He eventually left the company and formed a business partnership with another small, Black-owned company. For his experience and qualifications, it was a step down, but he took the job because he thought work would help him bury his problems. The new business caused even more stress, though—due to the company's size, he had to put in extra work just to earn a decent paycheck.

Meanwhile, my mother was adjusting to a new life on her own. For the first time ever, she was by herself, not to mention raising a teenage son and supporting two daughters. My parents' separation wasn't public, but people noticed. We still did things as a family—graduations, trips to Alabama, and other important events. When we were in public, my parents would be hand in hand. But the separation was real, and it stayed private for quite a while, until people started asking questions and prying. Those questions added another layer of stress—not just for my father but for the whole family.

With this recent change, my father added even more stress to his life. Meanwhile, all the medications he was taking for his health issues started to break his body down. His physical activity declined, and so did his appearance. The combination killed his urge to work out—he no longer biked, ran marathons, or played racquetball on weekends. The medicines and the condition of his heart, now weaker after two heart attacks, made all those things more difficult. While weight was never an issue for my father, you could still tell he was out of shape. Since he wasn't active anymore, he further buried himself in work, trying to escape his reality. He worked so much that it became visible in his appearance. It was a heartbreaking downfall. My father had always looked younger than he was; the only thing that gave away his age was a small, cool gray streak in his hair, just above his glasses on the left side. It made him look seasoned, not old, and the sparkle in his eyes made you feel comfortable the moment you met him. He was a sharp dresser, always turning heads when he walked into a room.

But with all the mess he was dealing with, that gray streak spread—each time I saw him, there was more gray in his hair. The light in his eyes dimmed. He was tired, beaten down by life; the stress was evident all over his face. Even with all of that, he was still "cool." He was still as social as he could be, managing to light up a room with just his personality. I don't know where he found the energy, but he always seemed to have it.

The stress led to more hospital visits—some overnight—and around that time, he always seemed to be sick. I saw him in the hospital so much that it started to feel routine, almost like something I would also inevitably face as I got older. Seeing him like that in his forties made me feel like I had to live life to the fullest before I reached forty, because then I, too, might be dealing with the problems he faced—and dealing with them often. The question "Is this my fate?" stuck with me from that moment. But I buried it, trying not to spend too much time thinking about it. I focused instead on the next big chapter in my life: high school.

8

D'Ville

The High School Years

The year was 2000. We made it past the Y2K bug scare without our computers crashing, which was a relief because people finally relaxed enough to be excited about the new millennium. Technology was evolving as cell phones became more common, and the first phone with a camera was released. Wi-Fi was developed, powering homes, businesses, and schools. And the PlayStation 2 was released, changing the gaming world forever! For me, I was just entering high school.

It had been nearly a year since my father had left the house, so I didn't see him as often. It was about once a week, as he would stop by the house occasionally for various things. But things still weren't settled between my parents. There were good days and days that weren't so good. It was all part of the process. But one thing that never died between them was the love. Yet, love didn't make the situation any easier, and it stressed Mom out quite a bit. It stressed her so much that my sister Shena moved back home to help out. My sister Jocelyn even started making arrangements to move closer to Ohio to be near us.

My parents' situation impacted the entire family, and we all dealt with it in our own way. Since my father was no longer at home, we started to lose focus on our healthier eating habits. We began to eat more of what was available rather than what was best for us. A lot of it was stress eating. According to Johns Hopkins Medicine, repeated and constant stressors, which elevate cortisol levels over a prolonged period, can lead to increased food consumption, fat storage, and weight gain. However, despite all the eating, I still didn't gain weight.

Despite everything going on, I tried to act as though everything was still normal. My mother tried to put me in therapy, but I felt I didn't need it, so I didn't cooperate. I felt like I didn't need to talk about my feelings. I wasn't "touched in the head," and how could we afford it anyway, since we weren't rich? To me, it was just life. Things happen, and it's not about what happened but what happens next. So I didn't spend too much time thinking about the situation. I buried it and any feelings associated with it. The only thing on my mind was surviving high school in D'Ville.

"D'ville!" is what the band would scream at our sporting events. It was a common nickname for Warrensville Heights. It was a way to reflect the pride and love we had for our school. High school was fun and exciting. From the band to the pride and the events, our school was like a historically Black college or university. We had step shows and fashion shows. There was always something going on, so I never needed an excuse to be at the high school.

I took it a day at a time. I also became more involved in activities. For instance, for the first two years, I was involved in our high school sports programs, but I didn't play sports. I always wanted to be helpful. That backfired one day when I signed up to be the manager of the women's freshman volleyball team; I didn't know that meant being the water boy. But I didn't mind because I was eager to help, not to mention I was around women for hours. I learned a great deal from them, and many of them remain my friends to this day. It's funny, looking back. For me, it was a way to stay active without fully joining the sports world. I had to attend every game, including away games, so I was just as involved in the season as the athletes. And I needed that distraction.

As the season went on, I met some upperclassmen volleyball players. My management even extended to the girls' basketball season. It allowed me to be around even more women outside my family, and talking to women older than me helped me overcome my shyness. As a sophomore, it even landed me the opportunity to go to homecoming with a senior! That was a real confidence booster for me. It even got me some cool points from my male friends.

I did all of this so I'd have a reason to be away from home. But there were still feelings I needed to release. My parents' situation never made me act out for attention, but I knew the stress was there, and I needed an outlet. So, instead of just helping with athletics, I eventually decided to play sports myself. With some convincing and the help of my father, we successfully persuaded my mother to let me join the football team during my junior year of high school. I made it! Playing football gave me the release I needed and woke up the competitive fire within me. As mentioned earlier, I was already an active kid, playing tag and tackle football with the neighborhood kids. So this was a natural next step, as many of the kids I had played with were already on the team.

This was one of the first times I can remember my father being proud of me. He would come and check out some of my practices, and even though he didn't live at the house, he missed only a few games. He was proud to brag that his son was on the football team. After the football season, I returned to help with the women's basketball team. I had built a bond with the coaching staff and players and didn't want to give that up.

Not only did I make the football team, but I also landed my very first job. I got hired at Panera Bread at sixteen. It was a way for me to help my mother out. I didn't want her to worry about me. Plus, I was saving up for my car. I picked up as many hours as I could while still playing football. I will admit it was a lot, and it took a toll on me. One of my favorite teachers always called me out for falling asleep in class. But I was in grind mode. I would wake up and be at school by 8 a.m. Right after school, I would head to football practice, and once that was over, I would rush home, shower, and go to work. These were thirteen-hour days for me. I even picked up track in my senior year. Like my father, I buried myself in busyness—school, sports, and work. It allowed me to escape my reality.

Despite the ongoing issues at home, the start of my senior year was a breath of fresh air. My social life was thriving, and I was granted more freedom than my sisters had ever experienced. While strict curfews had bound them, my mother was more lenient with me. I'm not sure if it was because of the issues she was dealing with regarding my father or simply because I was a boy. My senior year of football was big for me. I finally saved up enough to get a car. With everything I was doing, I needed it. It felt even better because I bought that car with the money I earned from Panera Bread. I called my 1994 blue Chevy Corsica "The Blue Mobile." I took a lot of pride in that car; it was the best seven hundred dollars I ever spent. Having a car allowed me to venture off and meet others outside my area. My adventures always included my best friends, Lamont and Nick. Lamont and I grew up together and have been tight since elementary school. Throughout the years, Lamont even joined me in helping out the women's sports teams. Nick entered the picture during our senior year. I met Nick during football practice. He had just transferred, and we connected quickly.

Nick's presence changed things for Lamont and me during our senior year. We usually spent most of our time in our neighborhood, hanging out with friends we knew from school. With all the kids in our neighborhood, we never needed to venture out and make new ones.

But when Nick came along, he had me all over the city, meeting lots of new people. I wasn't quite eighteen yet, so I frequently checked in with my mother, about once or twice a day, especially while on college visits. My mother was a worrier. I didn't get it then, but as an adult, I understand why she was worried. The world wasn't kind to young Black boys at the time. Plus, with her growing up in the South during the '60s, it was understandable that she was concerned whenever I was out in the world. My mother required frequent check-ins from me to calm her nerves.

Her compromise let me live out my teenage years without restrictions. Like any parent, she wanted to make sure she never got "that call": the call from a police station or an emergency room delivering terrible news that no parent wants to hear. It didn't help that Nick and I would do dumb stuff sometimes, just because we were young teenage boys. We weren't bad kids; we did nothing illegal, didn't drink heavily, or take any type of drugs. There were even some serious situations that we learned and grew from. But none of that helped my mother's anxiety. That's why checking in with her was crucial. It was the only thing allowing me to keep my freedom.

I was also in the process of selecting a college. If you know anything about the college admissions process, it starts as early as freshman year, and you should have a selection by the beginning of your senior year. That's how it usually works for most students. But not for me—I got a very late start. A lot of it was because I didn't know where to begin. I just felt that since my sisters went to school, I had to do the same. I knew I couldn't stay at home at eighteen. At that time, once you turned eighteen, you had to figure things out on your own. The options were college, a trade, or joining the military. I didn't inherit my grandfather's skills as a plasterer, and my mother wouldn't let her only son and youngest child join the military. Her nerves couldn't handle that.

Football is my only outlet, I thought. I never took my grades seriously. Additionally, Warrensville High wasn't known for its strong academics at the time. It felt like the goal was just to get us through high school, and if you went to college, that was merely a bonus. Our students usually got into college for two reasons: strong grades or participation in sports. So when it came time to make a college decision, football seemed like the only way. My mother would always tell me I was smart, but I thought she was supposed to say those things because she was my mom; I didn't believe it. My sisters made the dean's list and received various academic honors, something I failed to do, which made me feel like my options were limited during my college search. But honestly, I knew playing football made my father happy. Even in my mind, I thought this could be a way to get him home. So it only made sense to extend my playing career in college.

With the time spent at football games and other efforts to maintain appearances, I began to notice signs of progress with my parents. My sisters and I sensed that time was starting to heal old wounds. They wanted to reconcile, but something was holding them back. I did my part by making deals with my father to encourage his return. He was a huge baseball fan and had even played when he was younger. Although he tried to get me interested in it, it wasn't something I was into. Still, I offered to try out for the varsity baseball team if he came home. I was that confident in my athleticism. Most importantly, I wanted us to be a family again. But to be honest, I wasn't a superstar or high on anyone's recruitment list. I have my genetics to thank for my high school physique. In high school, I was much smaller than many of my classmates—around five feet six and 140 pounds. I played wide receiver on offense and cornerback on defense. Despite my size, I had decent speed and reliable hands. I never dropped a pass in a game.

While things were moving in the right direction, I noticed that my father wasn't in the stands for some of my games. This wasn't like him; he loved watching me play, even at practices. Those moments always made me feel good. We discussed the great moves I made and the areas I needed to improve. I was forming a new connection with my father through sports, which drew us closer. I had always viewed my dad as the man who told me what to do, disciplined me when I misbehaved, and protected me when I needed it. As a child, I never knew how to communicate with him other than to express my needs. However, during my journey to becoming a man, our conversations began to change and gain more depth. It became about more than my physical needs; it turned into what I needed to hear to grow. So, I noticed when he wasn't there at one of my games. But it wasn't just one game; it became several. Because while I was battling on the field, he was fighting for his life.

9

The Long Goodbye

It was a mild winter night in January 2004, 34 degrees with light snow covering the ground. I remember thinking it wasn't too bad outside—I had attended a party two nights prior without wearing a jacket. That stands out because during cold winter months, we tend to remember the warmer days. But the focus wasn't on the weather; it was on the fact that my father was finally home. He was back at the Warrensville house with his family, even some of my aunts from Alabama. Upon his return home, there was a lot of love in the moment. The overdue conversations between my parents, which included the words "I love you" and "I'm sorry," were all around. We were healing and finally coming together as a family. It was a moment of forgiveness, peace, and love. While I wish this were our happily-ever-after fairy-tale ending where love wins, that's not the case. This is because

my father's doctors gave him two weeks to live.

It all happened so quickly when I think about it now, but in the moment, the last days of my father's life felt like years were going by. It all started in late October 2003. We were in the middle of football season, and my dad had missed the last three games. I was beginning to wonder why, but I couldn't think of the words to say. My mind was on the upcoming college visits that I had planned to take with Nick.

Nick and I would usually schedule our college visits together, as we shared a dream of playing college ball together. We would meet the coaches and players and get a feel for different colleges and universities. Most of the time, we went on recruitment trips and drove to Columbus to stay with Nick's older brother. Most of the colleges were up to an hour and a half away, making it a relatively quick trip to and from Columbus.

I remember we purposely scheduled a round of recruitment visits right before Halloween weekend. We took time off from school and started visiting schools on Wednesday, staying until late Friday. It gave me the perfect excuse to have an extended weekend in Columbus, especially because Ohio University was hosting its annual Halloween party. OU is over an hour away from Columbus and hosts one of the nation's largest college parties. The event has seen crowds of upwards of ten thousand people. In some years, numbers have even exceeded thirty thousand. Attending a college party as high school seniors was the perfect way to end the trip. I won't go into too many details about the party, but I'll say the hype is real, which is why I went every year for seven years straight after my first visit. Coming off the high of my first college party, the harsh realities of life hit me quickly.

My mother and Jocelyn had agreed to take Nick and me back to Cleveland after our trip. I wasn't ready to tell my mother about the college party. Luckily, time was on my side, as I wasn't expecting to see Jocelyn until 5 p.m. In the meantime, I knew that my mother and sister wanted to spend some mother-daughter time together, starting with breakfast at Bob Evans. But before they even got seated, my mother received a phone call that threw everything off—not only for that day but for the rest of our lives. On the call, my mother was told,

"Sam has been rushed to the hospital."

There weren't many details, but with his health history and issues, she knew it was serious. My mother never took any chances or brushed things off as false alarms. With as many health events as my father had, we couldn't afford to do that—especially when this marked the fourth major hospital visit in under ten years. Immediately after hearing the news, my mother called me and told me we needed to return to Cleveland right away. She told me my father was in the hospital, but I just felt relieved that this news distracted her and she wasn't thinking about how I had spent that weekend. I know it may sound cruel, but that was on my mind. I was just used to my father being in the hospital at this point. I had started to become numb to it. I don't remember being worried or scared. My mindset differed from that of my mother and sisters. I remember thinking, *Dad has been in the hospital so many times; it's routine by now.* This was how I mostly remembered my father while growing up, starting when I was eight years old. Now, at seventeen, it was simply a normal part of my life, which was a problem because I was normalizing my trauma.

According to the *Millennium Journal of Health*, in communities that normalize trauma—especially marginalized ones—our minds are wired to prioritize survival. We learn to bury the pain just to keep going. For me, the trauma wasn't physical; it was mental. My parents' separation and its impact on the family were significant. So were my father's frequent hospital visits. It was like I was watching my dad deteriorate in front of my eyes. The memory of the handsome, charming, intelligent Southern boy faded as my everyday reality became a man who bore the weight of the world on his shoulders. I was also dealing with the pressures of growing up and trying to be as normal as possible. Yet, I didn't have a dad around all the time to ask about girls, how to deal with certain situations, or other advice a young man would ask his dad. People were noticing my father was no longer in the household. That perfect image we tried to keep up could only last so long. By now, he had been away from the house for about four years. Even with all this going on, I never addressed it. I just continued to live life as I thought a person my age should. But in the back of my head, I always thought I would share the same fate.

Because my sister and mother were already in Columbus, that helped cut the two-hour drive to Cleveland a bit. But time was of the essence. We needed to be there for Dad in his time of need. Jocelyn coordinated with Nick's brother to arrange a pickup thirty miles outside Columbus. He got us there as fast as he could. It was a quick exchange at a gas station off the highway. Despite being polite and smiling, my mother and sister's fear was apparent.

Thoughts about my dad's condition fueled my sister, who was driving. During the drive home, my mother was getting constant updates from Shena, who was at the hospital with Dad. After each call, my mom would give us updates, but the ride was otherwise silent. It felt like my sister switched lanes every two seconds, avoiding the cars that were moving too slowly. Luckily, there weren't many cops out that day, and Jocelyn got us back to Cleveland in an hour and fifteen minutes.

Once we arrived back in the city and dropped Nick off, we went straight to the hospital. Few details were available, but his illness was serious. He had so many machines and tubes attached, and he was visibly weak. Yet another mental image of my father lying in a hospital bed and losing parts of himself. This time differed from other hospital stays because the doctors feared he wouldn't bounce back from this. The doctors ran every type of test on him to try to determine the source of his illness, but they never found it. All they could say was that an unknown infection had attacked his body. They admitted my father to a hospital partnered with a local medical school. Doctors would bring students around to explain what they knew of his case. They would take pictures of him and strange things on his body that they couldn't identify. I felt like my dad was an exhibit. As my father was fighting to get better, his sickness amazed them.

While my father was in the hospital, football season was still in progress. Up until then, every Friday, I could look in the stands and find my family, including my mother and father, sitting together in a show of support. However, that wasn't the case anymore. Still, that didn't stop me from bringing football to him. One day during a visit, I surprised my dad with the Coach's Award I had won for the season. He was out of it most of the time, but when he saw that award, he woke up and lit up. It was good to see that familiar spark in his eyes once again. He couldn't talk, but I knew what he felt, and I know he would have said he was proud of me.

This time, Dad stayed in the hospital longer than usual because the doctors still didn't know how to treat him. But it was to his benefit, as he appeared to get much better than expected, though he still had a long way to go. His improvement prompted a transfer to a rehabilitation center. The rehab center differed from the hospital. It was about thirty minutes away from Warrensville. On the drive, I would faithfully play Jay-Z's *The Black Album* from start to finish. The album matched perfectly with the landmarks I would see on my journey. If I were on 270 North, "Justify My Thug" would play, followed by "My 1st Song." It never failed and became routine.

When I would arrive to see my father, he would be asleep most of the time. He was too weak to have regular conversations, so most visits were silent. But it was still quality time spent together. Although unspoken, my father understood and valued my support. Sometimes I would talk to him, knowing he wouldn't respond, but it still meant a lot to me to be able to just talk with my father. I was sharing more of my coming-of-age issues with him. As a senior in high school, I was meeting new people, starting serious relationships, and thinking about major life decisions. I would usually visit my father during the day, around 2 to 3 p.m. My stays were short due to football practice and other sporting events I assisted with. Plus, I was still working at Panera. I would be at work after practice or at sporting events on off days.

There was always love and support around my father. My mother and father had more time to talk and move on to the next chapter in their lives. When we learned my father was going to get out of the hospital, he and my mother agreed that he would move back into the house. Whatever issues they had before, they actively planned to work through them and be a family. That motivated the entire family to push a bit harder for him to get home. So, the New Year's resolution for my parents was to get the family back together.

But things turned quickly, and for the worse, a little after the new year of 2004. One night in early January, the rehabilitation center called with bad news: My dad had caught a severe case of pneumonia. Since his body was already in a weakened state, it took such a toll that he most likely would not recover from it. We had heard this before, but it was different this time. Doctors predicted he had about two weeks left to live, and they arranged for accommodations so he could spend his last days comfortably at home in hospice. We got our dad back, but this wasn't how we had expected it.

But as always, we are a praying family. We gave it to God and asked for a miracle. It didn't help that when they sent my father home, they cut off some of the essential medicines he needed to survive. To the doctors, there was no need for it, and paying for medicines would be a waste at that point. All he had were ventilators and other machines to assist with breathing. He didn't have medicines that fought cholesterol, helped proper heart function, or managed blood pressure. His body would have to fight that on its own.

But in those last two weeks of his life, my father had many visitors come and see him at the house. His family from Alabama came up to be with him and help the family. His Cleveland coworkers and church members came to pay their last respects and offer their final words of comfort. One of the most memorable moments was when his Kappa Alpha Psi fraternity brothers came over and talked about those college days and fraternity life. They even did a step and stroll to lift his spirits. In the Black Greek world known as the Divine Nine, stepping and strolling are synchronized group dances, unique to each fraternity/sorority, that showcase pride and history at parties, step shows, and competitions.

And it did lift his spirits; he was highly engaged and in the moment. The love and support were overwhelming. Despite his weakness in bed, he felt it deeply, and his eyes sparkled. That energy filled my father with more life. See, love was all he needed, we thought as he improved. You could see that light in his eyes once again, and he was attempting to become more vocal. But the funny thing about death is that it often arrives unexpectedly; being a praying family, we expected a miracle in answer to our prayers. Since my father was so full of life, as much as he could be, we thought we would have that miracle. We thought the Lord heard our prayers and would provide a powerful testimony because the world needed my father. And most of all, our family had unfinished business, and we were so close to our happily ever after.

On Thursday night, January 21, 2004, the power in the house shut off out of nowhere. There were no storms or reported outages in the area, which led to confusion. This was the worst possible thing at that moment because life-support machinery kept my father with us. We did not know what to do, which led to panic. We needed to regain power as soon as possible! Thankfully, my uncle was there and knew to check the circuit breakers, which were the issue because of a power overload. After we reset the breakers and restored power, the machines took some time to reload. During all of this, my father's breathing changed. It sounded like every breath he took was an effort. He was gasping for air. I'll never forget that sound—it sounded so painful, like he was fighting for his life.

When the power went out, it wiped out the improvements and good spirits he'd shown over the last few weeks. My mother sat by his side, helpless and in pain, as she had to witness her husband of thirty years fight to take what could be his last breaths. But nobody wanted to admit it, as we still prayed that he would pull through and that this was just a slight setback.

After the power had been back on for a bit and the family had calmed down a little, I took some time to have a moment with him. His breathing wasn't as loud, the breaths were slower, and he was calmer. But something told me to take this moment now. I don't remember the exact words, but I do know I told him I loved him. While I was still optimistic and thought he would make it, I wanted him to know and hear that from me. Like all the other times I visited him in the hospitals and rehabilitation centers, I wanted him to know I was still there.

Even after this tense evening, I still had school the next day. I had to keep things as routine as possible to stay on track, compartmentalizing and normalizing everything that was going on at home and in school life. I accepted it all as my life. So even after that scary moment, I still thought I would be going to school the next day, and I needed to start my nightly routine: taking a shower, laying out my clothes, and mentally preparing for the next day. Since the power had gone out earlier, I got a later start than usual, so I didn't get to shower until a little after midnight. About five minutes into my shower, there was a knock at the door. I remember feeling irritated because this was the first moment I had had to decompress from the day's stress. Before I could even respond, I heard the door open and the voice of my sister Jocelyn. I'll never forget what she said:

"Hey, we think Dad just took his last breath…"

January 22, 2004, is the day my father passed away. The doctors were right. It was two weeks from when he left the rehabilitation center to his death. While we knew this was coming, we weren't prepared for it to happen. We are a praying family. We were supposed to get a miracle! Had the power never gone out, would he still be here? What could we have done differently? Those were the questions swirling around as we waited for the funeral home to come pick up the body. There were hugs, heavy as bodies broke down from the weight of sadness. Tears-soaked shirts as people leaned on each other's shoulders. There were looks of disbelief that he was gone.

A couple of weeks later, we held a small celebration-of-life service for him back in Northport. Family, close friends, and fraternity brothers shared stories and memories of my dad. So many people had great memories of my father. After the service, we fulfilled his wish to spread his ashes across his parents' graves and across the Valley where he grew up. We kept some of his ashes for ourselves, including a cross with his ashes that I still have to this day.

On January 22, my father was released from his suffering. No more pain, no more stress. During his last days, he was surrounded by a great deal of love. He was at his house. His wife and children were by his side, along with extended family members. Within those two weeks, people paid their respects, said their goodbyes, and shared their love for my father and our family. All past issues, troubles, and problems didn't matter at that moment. The only thing that mattered was the love, laughter, and positive memories we shared with my father. We also witnessed firsthand how stress sped up his health problems. We can sit and wonder if things would have turned out differently if we had addressed certain things earlier, if he had managed his stress differently, if he'd had more time to seek therapy to address issues from childhood, if he'd continued to work out and stay active even when things seemed tense, and, finally, if he'd taken his health treatment more seriously after his initial diagnosis. All we can do is learn from his mistakes, cherish his life and memories, and, most of all, appreciate that he found peace on Earth during his journey to heaven.

After my father's death, each family member coped in different ways. My mother grieved deeply, struggling with the loss. Being separated is one thing, but losing a partner is entirely different. My sister Shena supported our mother through her grief. My sister Jocelyn began her law career and became serious with her longtime boyfriend, who she had met in Iowa during college. Meanwhile, I finished my senior year and narrowed down my college choices. I finally made my decision with a school I instantly fell in love with. In college, I created incredible memories with lifelong friends. However, I also lost focus and started developing habits that would eventually catch up to me when I least expected.

10

Midnight McGriddle Madness

The College Years

In 2003, just before I started college, McDonald's released what I still consider one of its best items ever: the McGriddle. The perfect combination of pancake buns and savory fillings like bacon or sausage, egg, and cheese makes it one of the best breakfast sandwiches I've ever had. The only drawback is that it is only available during breakfast hours. In high school, I had to be at school early and never had a chance to grab one on my way to class. But everything changed when I got to college. It was the first time I'd seen a twenty-four-hour location. The concept of being able to get food at any hour was surreal. Since it was open around the clock, they switched to breakfast at 3 a.m. With my lively group of roommates and a car, this was the recipe for several terrible eating habits and adventures that set the stage for my future health issues.

Although my eating habits weren't the best, my college years were incredible. It was one of the greatest periods of my life, and I have no regrets. I didn't reinvent myself, but it felt like a fresh start—mostly because I was moving away from the recent grief of my father's passing. Leaving all that behind was necessary and healing. I was now in a new place, making new friends, and figuring a lot out on my own. Through it all, I stayed true to myself. I came to realize that blood isn't the only thing that makes you family; experiences, connection, and love are just as important. While appreciating the family I already had, I also learned to be wise in choosing friends who would become like family. I began my radio career while at college, which blossomed into a meaningful career for years afterward. Only at my university could I have done these things—my experience there truly shaped who I am.

Ohio Dominican University, or ODU, became my school of choice. My friend Nick told me they were starting a football team, and since I wanted to continue playing, I looked into it. ODU is a small Catholic university in Columbus near the airport and five miles from Ohio State University. With a student population of around 2,700 at the time, it was mostly a commuter school. The Dominican Sisters of St. Mary of the Springs, later known as the Dominican Sisters of Peace, founded ODU (not to be confused with the Dominican Republic—that's a question I heard a lot!). The Dominican Sisters are a Catholic religious order, and education is one of their main ministries.

Having attended public school, the idea of going to a Catholic college never crossed my mind until I visited. On my first tour, I was struck by the beauty of the campus. Nick and I had visited several others just before this tour, but ODU stood out from the rest. Throughout every step of the admissions process, ODU was responsive and personable—they made me feel valued and appreciated. My high school grades were just barely good enough, but my test scores helped. Most schools would have just moved on, but ODU was different. They helped me, recommended tests to boost my application, and encouraged me to stick with it. It worked, and I started at ODU in fall 2004.

The school felt large during class hours, thanks to the big commuter population, though only about four hundred students lived on campus. Most of those were from Columbus or nearby, so being from out of town really made you stand out. Since the school had an average class size of seventeen, I had the opportunity to get to know my classmates and receive the personalized attention I needed. I loved asking questions and knew I wouldn't have thrived at a huge school. ODU is considered nontraditional, with many students who were older or working full-time. That exposed me to classmates from all backgrounds. Minority enrollment stood at 32 percent, so in a typical class of seventeen, there would likely be five students of color. Coming from Warrensville, with 98 percent Black students, this helped me feel more comfortable. While the number wasn't as high as at some nearby schools, it mattered.

My main goal at college was to continue playing football, and ODU was in its first season in 2004. All of us—the incoming freshmen and transfers—were starting with a clean slate, so I thought I'd have a shot. But due to my conditional acceptance, I had to sit out my first year. That turned out to be a blessing because it freed me to join the college radio station.

I joined RadiODU, the student-run radio station, in my freshman year. Once I got involved, football faded into the background as radio became my focus. By sophomore year, I was hired as station manager, and during my time, we expanded the radio station and covered more events. We called football, soccer, volleyball, and basketball games; played music over the air and around campus; and made sure I, DJ-SP, was always in the mix.

Some of my best friends in life emerged from those years—people like Lindsey Weed, an unexpected friend from my days at Panera Bread who also attended Ohio Dominican. Weed, as we called her, was also a reminder of home, as the only person I knew before attending the university. When seasonal breaks came along, we would always stuff my car with bags and hit the road to come home together.

Nick V. was my suitemate for a while and became my radio broadcasting partner—we called sports games together, with him on play-by-play and me as the color commentator. We had no clue what we were doing, but we always had fun. My longest roommate outside of my family, James Lee (J. Lee), was also from Cleveland. We met through my high school friend Nick (not Nick V.), and we instantly connected. Rooming together was one of my best choices. J. Lee wasn't just a roommate; he became a brother. Two young Black men from Cleveland, we navigated college together, always looking out for one another. J. Lee was the best man at my wedding, and we're still best friends today.

One of the most formative experiences was joining a fraternity, as my dad had. Although I was conflicted about continuing his legacy, I followed my heart and joined Alpha Phi Alpha Fraternity. Alpha was a turning point, changing my approach to life. For the first time, I was surrounded by older Black men outside my family who could mentor me. I gained brothers—not just fraternity brothers, but my line brothers Andrew, Desmond, and PJ. Going through the centennial year of our fraternity wasn't easy, but we held each other down and remain close two decades later.

Alpha was a blessing I hadn't expected. During high school, family distractions kept me from asking my dad those crucial man-to-man questions, but Alpha filled that gap. Now, I had a network of brothers of all ages, abilities, and professions—people who pushed me to grow. They showed me how to dress and present myself, encouraged me to level up, taught me how to use influence for positive change, and helped me understand the principles of leadership. Fraternity life opened up new social circles across the state since our chapter included students from surrounding colleges. I met people everywhere, visited other universities, and made friends throughout the city.

When I mentioned life-threatening habits earlier, it probably isn't what you think. It wasn't drinking or drugs (I actually kept my D.A.R.E. pledge) or womanizing, despite the rumors about "frat boys." No, my problem was careless, reckless eating. While most freshmen fear the "Freshman Fifteen," I never worried about it. I stayed active with intramural sports, so my physical appearance never reflected the damage I was doing internally.

My environment didn't help. The campus was small with limited dining options, so I couldn't exactly explore gourmet choices. Hamilton Hall, the main dining facility, always offered a traditional "home-cooked" dish like meatloaf or spaghetti alongside the fast-food staples. But since I was a picky eater, I ignored the home-cooked options and devoured pizza, burgers, and fries nearly every day, especially during Lent when they didn't serve meat on Fridays.

Panther Plaza, just below the radio station, offered quick snacks and subs, but it closed at 5 p.m. and wasn't open on weekends, as it was more for commuters than residents. The Underground, my favorite, was the late-night option. They served more burgers, fries, chicken tenders, and pizza, plus had pool tables, TVs, and a laid-back vibe. We often hung out there until midnight.

When we ventured off campus, Columbus, being a college town, offered more food choices than I'd ever imagined. I saw more twenty-four-hour drive-throughs than I had ever seen before. As a top test market city with over ten colleges, Columbus was the perfect setup for brands to try new menu items. Since I was one of the few freshmen with a car, I could go anywhere, anytime.

This brings me back to the twenty-four-hour McDonald's just two minutes from ODU on Cassady Avenue. Some of my most lasting college memories feature late-night McDonald's runs. Whether grabbing food after a party or picking up snacks for the big brothers of Alpha,

McDonald's was a staple. During our sophomore year, J. Lee and I shared a suite with Oba (from Detroit) and Ju (from Chicago). Rooming with friends made everyday life feel like an endless sleepover. Our place became the campus hangout, with people always stopping by. People like our friend Dori, who quickly became a part of the crew, even joining us on our late-night food runs. During our late nights, we realized that when the clock neared 3 a.m., it was McGriddle time.

We'd leave a few minutes before the menu switched and be the first in line. Going so often, we got to know the workers—and they knew us too. Sometimes we mixed things up and went to Waffle House, a rare treat for me since there weren't many in Cleveland. Between campus visits and late-night cravings, I tried every open spot—like Raising Cane's near Ohio State, which stayed open until 4 a.m. Pizza was always an option as well. I could get whatever I wanted, whenever I wanted.

For once in my life, I had "McDonald's money," and it was great.

But it was also my downfall. You'd think after losing my father, I'd have been more careful. Instead, I ignored my health. With no parents to say no to fast food or remind me to eat vegetables, I did whatever I wanted. Things got so bad that I kept an industrial-sized ketchup pump in my room to drown my fries. My cholesterol diagnosis meant nothing then. With no close family in Columbus, home-cooked meals were only available when I visited home or went to Grandma's for Thanksgiving. Things didn't improve after college. By then, it was nearly impossible to break the deadly cycle. While I didn't notice the effects at first, the damage had begun. Eating whatever and whenever, with no balance, led to an unchecked buildup of cholesterol—my "good" HDL may have been high before, but all the fast food and mindless choices piled up the danger. It got much worse before it ever got better in the next phase of my journey.

II

It Was the Best of Times, It Was the Worst of Times

One of my late father-in-law's favorite quotes, from Charles Dickens's *A Tale of Two Cities*, perfectly sums up my life after college: "It was the best of times, it was the worst of times." I stayed in Columbus after graduation and didn't move back home, so I was alone. I had an apartment, enjoyed life as an adult, and—most importantly—landed my dream job! But that all changed when my sister put things into perspective. I was living in poverty, which played a massive part in my health and nutrition. Believe it or not, my diet actually got worse than it was even in college.

During college, after pledging Alpha, I had a wake-up call. Being part of Alpha instilled a sense of pride and helped me realize I was a leader on my campus, which included being a scholar. I began to focus more on my studies and grades, applying myself seriously for the first time. It paid off—I graduated from ODU in four years. Those four years flew by, yet I had no idea what I was doing after school. I never applied for internships. I never worked at an external radio station during my college years. My summer jobs included being a nanny and working at a hotel, both roles that helped pay for my education. In a way, I just didn't have time for an internship because I needed to earn money. As graduation crept up, I had no plans to return to Cleveland, so I needed to figure things out quickly.

All I knew was that it was my destiny to have a career in radio. Thankfully, my experience with RadiODU saved me. Right before I graduated, I met a young man who worked at the local hip-hop radio station. Excited to meet him, I eagerly asked if he could put in a word for me if I applied. "Yeah, no doubt; just drop my name when you apply," he replied. His name was Yaves, and it's hard to forget a name like that. When he said that, I really believed him. But when I applied, it didn't turn out how I'd hoped. They had no positions open. They told me they'd keep my résumé on file and would call if something opened up.

Discouraged by the news, reality set in: I needed to find a real job. I didn't know what that looked like. Outside of radio, what was I supposed to do? At least I had a degree, I reasoned, so I might as well apply for some entry-level jobs. I had options, but nothing felt right. Everything else still seemed like a waste of time because I knew what I truly wanted. But I had bills, rent, and living expenses. During college, my work-study job and savings had been enough, but now that wasn't a viable source. I was slowly coming to terms with the idea that working as a manager-in-training at the car rental place might be my best move. But God had other plans.

I had just finished my second interview for the car rental job, and it went well. Before fully accepting that my radio career might be over before it began, something prompted me to call the radio station and check on the status of my application. Even though they had nothing open, I wanted them to know how serious I was, so I followed up. "Hello, sir," I said nervously, trying to impress the hiring manager. "I applied for the remote tech job; I just wanted to see if you got my application." Honestly, I didn't even know what a remote tech was. I just wanted to get my foot in the door. "Aah, Sam, yes, we did. What time works for you to come in and talk?" the hiring manager replied. *Wait, what? A couple of weeks ago there was nothing, and now they want me to come in?* Was this a dream?

It turned out to be true. One of the remote techs had taken a job with another company, and they needed a replacement. I'll never forget going to the station in a full suit and tie while the hiring manager wore a T-shirt and jeans. I didn't care—I wanted them to see how serious I was. And it worked. I got hired and launched the next part of my radio journey with Radio One. When I met my future boss, he said, "Any friend of Yaves is a friend of ours. Welcome aboard." Yaves was right: Just by mentioning his name, all my lack of experience was overlooked. All that mattered was being a friend of Yaves.

It was indeed the best of times. I was living a dream and learning new things every day. But in my eagerness to be part of the company, I hadn't paid enough attention to a few crucial details. I quickly learned what part-time really meant and faced the true implications of the pay. I was earning minimum wage—seven dollars an hour in Ohio at the time. I didn't mind; as long as the bills were paid, I was happy. Living with my line brother Des helped with expenses, but I was only making between five hundred and eight hundred dollars a month, and even that wasn't consistent. We were limited by hours, but I became indispensable because I was there every day, learning fast. Even though they wanted to cut my hours, they couldn't, because I handled every-thing—promos, production, office work, and even being on air during the third shift. Any hour, any day, you'd find me at the station. I had full-time responsibilities in a part-time position.

My living expenses were about four hundred dollars, leaving me with one hundred to four hundred dollars left over. I didn't party much outside work events or take trips. Really, all my money went to bills and food. I couldn't afford anything else, and that was okay because I was always at the station. Being there constantly meant I had no time for grocery shopping or cooking, so fast food became my everyday food choice.

My biggest mistake was thinking there wasn't enough time to cook, which was partially true. I was at the station from 9 a.m. to 4 p.m. every day, then back from 7 p.m. until 11 p.m. or later to watch the night show. In between, it was always quicker and cheaper to grab something to go. But the real reason I didn't cook? I didn't know how. The only dishes I could make were spaghetti, tacos, and fried chicken. I'd mention cooking eggs, but I couldn't even do those right. So my idea of a home-cooked meal meant either one of those things or just a microwave dinner. Sad part: I actually "seasoned" those microwave dinners, not realizing how much salt they already contained. Many frozen meals contain high sodium—sometimes more than the daily recommendation in a single serving. I was buying "family meals" just for myself. I would take a peek at the food labels, not caring what they said, but it was always a slight nod to Mrs. Dunning. If she knew how many calories I was consuming then, she would have been disappointed. Because between the ages of twenty-two and twenty-five,

I consumed approximately 3,000 to 4,500 calories daily.

It feels surreal to say that, but let me explain. Most days, I skipped breakfast, heading straight to the station. Around noon, I'd drive with coworkers to get lunch. I still had that college mindset, so it was always burgers and fries for me—always large fries, because I loved them. McDonald's was still the go-to: a large Filet-O-Fish meal with Sprite, totaling 1,410 calories. For my second meal around 6 p.m.—usually after returning from the station—I'd microwave a chicken fettuccine alfredo meal. That alone was 460 calories and 890 mg of sodium before I added more salt. I always added more. Not just regular salt—seasoning salt too. For drinks, I was big on fruit juice: around 70 calories a cup, easily multiplied by four because I'd refill my cup often. Later at night, back at the station, I'd always have something else—maybe Wendy's for variety. That might be ten nuggets (450 calories), BBQ sauce (90), a Junior Bacon Cheeseburger (310), Biggie Fries (510), and a Biggie Sprite (250). Adding all that up, that's 3,760 calories on a "cook at home" day. Many days, it was fast food for lunch, dinner, and after work. And with working the third shift, my schedule—and my eating—was totally thrown off.

The wild thing: My eating still didn't affect my physique. I stayed active during this time because many of my friends were still in school, and I would often play pickup basketball with them. The radio station's hours were flexible, making it easy to socialize or be active. I joined basketball and flag football leagues, which counted as my exercise. This masked just how bad my diet really was—as I said, it was worse than college. Unlike ODU, where the buffet would sometimes surprise you with a normal, healthy option—such as vegetables or fruit—my only veggies now were iceberg lettuce and tomatoes.

Sometimes, the voices of my mother and Mrs. Dunning, along with the memory of my father's struggle, would echo in my head, encouraging me to eat healthily. But healthy meals just left me unsatisfied. Still hungry. But that's an illusion—when you're used to eating badly, you end up compromising the quality of your food and making malnutrition worse—what the World Health Organization calls "hidden hunger." Hidden hunger is a kind of malnutrition that shows up when you don't get the vitamins and minerals your body really needs, even if you're full. When shopping for food on a slim budget, you just buy what fills you up.

As strange as it sounds, this wasn't so unusual: In 2008, 13.2% of Americans lived at or below poverty levels. Blinded by dreams and enjoying the best times at work and in my social life, I never realized I was living in poverty until my sister pointed it out at tax time. Shena has our father's gift for numbers, and since I couldn't afford anyone else, I was lucky that she helped with my taxes. After my second year at the station, she looked at my finances and said,

"You have a college degree and live in poverty."

That was a wake-up call. I didn't immediately connect it to my eating habits, but it did prompt me to think. Four years in private Catholic school for my bachelor's, and here I was living like I hadn't even finished high school. When I heard it, it felt like I might have been better off dropping out much earlier and diving right into a career in radio. What did I really have to show for college? Was it a waste of time and money? Those questions stuck with me. Her words motivated me more than she realized—and looking back, they might have even saved my life.

That uncertainty reminds me of the wisdom my father-in-law lived by. Even though it was years before I met him, looking back now, I can still find peace hearing his voice in my ear, reassuring me through the doubt:

"It's gon be alright."

The Prediction
My Second Warning

"You won't live to see thirty"—six words I will never forget. Those words hit me hard at age twenty-six, igniting fear and uncertainty in my mind. They lingered before and after my heart attack, a constant reminder of my mortality. Considering my eating habits at that time and what I know now, I understand how the doctor genuinely believed what she said. It took me a while to admit it, but she wasn't wrong. Timing is everything. The ironic part is that I went to the doctor that day for allergy and sinus issues. The last thing I wanted to hear about was my cholesterol, something I had been aware of for nearly half my life by then. I wasn't prepared to accept that message. In fact, it turned me off. I shut down and remember nothing else she said. Part of it was the mistrust of the medical system creeping into my mind, but most of the reasons I didn't respond well were merely excuses.

During a visit to my alma mater to attend to some business, I ended up with a job offer. I ran into someone who had worked in the admissions office while I was in college. Her name was Nicole, and she is unforgettable. She was always so cheerful and full of energy. It had only been two years since I graduated, so I still felt a strong connection to the university and its staff. When she asked how I was doing, I replied,

"Well, are y'all hiring?" I said it jokingly, but I was somewhat serious about it. This came just after my sister mentioned that I was living on a poverty-level wage. As luck would have it, they were hiring, and she was the boss. Since my graduation, she had been promoted to director of admissions and was now searching for a new admissions counselor.

It was the perfect job for me for several reasons. First, I got to talk, which is something I love doing. Better yet, I got to discuss my college experience. I truly appreciated my time at the university, and it was the perfect way to relive some great memories. I wanted others to have the same experience I did, and that motivated me. The second reason is that Nicole was well aware that my heart was with radio. I never quit the station; I just reduced my hours. I mainly spent time at the station after regular work hours and on weekends. Knowing my passion, Nicole accommodated my radio schedule and encouraged me in my radio career. I learned many valuable lessons from her, and I appreciate her for that and for taking a chance on me.

With this job, I finally saw a real paycheck for the first time. I went from wishing I could work enough hours to earn four hundred dollars per check to tripling that amount. You might think that, with better pay, I would improve my diet because I could now afford better food options; that wasn't the case. Instead, I ate the same things at higher prices, moving from a fast-food burger to a steakhouse burger.

Balancing my radio career with my ODU job kept me away constantly—like the days when I juggled high school, football, and work. ODU was my moneymaker, my nine-to-five that kept the bills paid. Right after, I'd have an hour and a half to head home, maybe nap, then get ready for the radio. I'd hit the station by 6:30 and wouldn't leave until midnight. Every day felt like that movie *Groundhog Day*—my daily routine until the fall travel season hit.

Travel season for college admissions counselors meant college fairs across the state, where we'd line up to be the smiling face swaying a kid's final college choice. I covered twenty-eight of Ohio's eighty-eight counties—our biggest territory. Constant road time killed healthy eating. Visiting Cleveland in Cuyahoga County, home to the state's most high schools, meant days at Mom's for home-cooked meals served with love. She lit up seeing me since I was rarely around. But those visits were short—I'd hit the road for the other twenty-seven counties: more fast food, desk time, car hours, and weight gain.

On the road, I always tried to get food options I couldn't get anywhere else because if it was a popular food chain, I most likely already had it for dinner a night or two ago. ODU reimbursed me 100 percent of the business expenses I incurred. "Spend it like it's your own money," Nicole would say. That was no problem for me, as I was accustomed to the low prices of fast food. Instead of going to higher-quality restaurants, I would order the larger meal plus another side item to accompany it, thereby increasing my intake of calories, salt, trans fats, and harmful ingredients.

With so much traveling and the long work hours, I no longer had the time to work out. Instead, in my free time, I started to pick up more social drinking. I had never been a drinker before, but catching up with friends I no longer saw as much became an escape from my hectic days. When I was least expecting it, the weight of my decisions caught up with me. I mean that literally.

I noticed myself getting bigger and out of shape for the first time. I noticed all the bad eating, drinking, and lack of physical activity in my appearance. That was new for me. My entire life, I'd been this skinny kid, but now I was packing on some extra pounds, and it didn't look as good as I had thought it would. When I was younger, I used to pray for additional weight. It didn't come then, but it was here now. It reminded me of two things. First, God's not always there when you call, but he's always on time. Second, be careful what you pray for.

The best thing about my job with ODU was the benefits. I was fully covered, with very few occasions to have to pay out of pocket for anything. We didn't even have any deductions come out of our paychecks. Before I started my job at ODU, I didn't visit the doctor often. I didn't feel it was necessary. I was very active and seemed to maintain a healthy weight, so I convinced myself I didn't need to go. Due to that deep mistrust of the medical system, I only sought help when something was wrong or when over-the-counter medicine couldn't fix the issue.

For example, before working at ODU, I had broken a bone and still didn't think to go to the doctor to get it properly checked out. During a game in one of my competitive football leagues, I jumped and landed right on my hand. At the time, it didn't seem too bad, aside from some manageable pain. When I woke up, I found that my hand was twice its usual size. It was more serious than I had realized. But I still didn't think to go to the doctor. After seeing my hand's size, anyone else would have gone and had it checked out immediately, but not me; my coworkers had to convince me to go. For transparency, I did have benefits. I was under twenty-six, so I was still under my mother's insurance at the time. But still, I didn't have any money for the copay, and I wasn't sure if I could fully trust what they would say. But with such excellent benefits from ODU, I decided to address my sinus issues at least and finally have a long-overdue physical.

My appointment was scheduled for Tuesday, September 18, 2012. I hadn't had a primary care doctor in years. I would usually visit urgent care centers around the city if I needed any care. But this time was different because I had benefits, and I had to stay in the network to get the best rates. I visited the Ohio State University Wexner Medical Center, which is regarded as one of the top medical centers in the area. I got checked in with no issues, but I had to answer hundreds of questions since they didn't have any medical history on file for me: questions about family history, drug abuse, if I felt safe, and if I had fallen in the last six months. I was pretty honest, even about my cholesterol situation. After I completed the paperwork, a nurse took me to a room and checked my vitals. She let me know the doctor would be in in a few minutes.

The doctor walked in and extended her hand for a shake as she introduced herself. She wasn't what I was expecting. She was a young white woman who appeared to be my age. At one point, I wondered if I might have seen her around Ohio State's campus. But that couldn't have been the case. All signs pointed to her being a fully practicing doctor, not an attending or resident. Still, her youthful appearance threw me off. Stereotypically, I was used to older individuals being doctors, which made me skeptical.

I got tested for everything during my visit. The results took some time, so the doctor asked about my medical history. I remember it being an uncomfortable feeling for me. It may have been the age perception, but it prevented me from being open and honest with the doctor. I still ran down a list of what was bad and good and what I could do better. All the while, I was trying to convince the doctor that I was in good shape. During the middle of my pitch, we received the test results. I was instantly proven wrong. I had mentioned my high cholesterol, but now she saw how serious it was. She looked at me with a serious yet stunned face and said,

"Whoa, I have never seen anybody with cholesterol as high as yours at your age."

In my mind, I had a "duh" moment. I had mentioned it was high, but I realized she wasn't expecting it to be this high. Still, I didn't think it was as serious as she made it out to be. I had lived with this for years and felt fine. But her following words were the six words that changed my life forever. She continued to say:

"You won't live to see thirty."

I was offended because now I felt I was being threatened with death, and I didn't take it well. When I replay that moment in my mind, I remember the message being delivered in a cold, emotionless way. That made me shut down. While I was processing her words, I was trying to determine if I was right to be offended or if I should be sad that I was told I was going to die in the next three years. Was it a scare tactic or a legit diagnosis? It eventually became a horrible experience simply because my feelings were hurt. But my pride made me believe it was due to bad bedside manners.

Bedside manners are important and could be the difference between life and death. For all the concerns about the health care industry, bedside manners are high on the list. According to a systematic review of patient-physician communication studies, "Race-related attitudes among physicians, even if held implicitly, may influence the quality of communication in patient-physician interactions and thus impact the disparities in treatment and information exchange." An article from the law firm Freedland Harwin Gander Valori, which handles medical malpractice, states, "Bad bedside manners can cause a patient to ex-perience a lack of compassion, respect, or understanding from a health care professional." I will always remember this moment as an example of bad bedside manner. I reflect on that day as the first time that I was called out as an adult and reminded of how dangerous high cholesterol levels can be.

I never confirmed whether it was a matter of feelings or a lack of compassion because I never saw that doctor again. Truth be told, I didn't care. I didn't take the threat of death well. Then again, she was the first doctor in years to be in the position to deliver the hard, cold facts, which doesn't make her the bad guy in the situation. But her warning was enough to make me follow up with the lipid specialist she referred me to due to my high cholesterol. At first, I thought about skipping the visit because I was still upset about it. But I decided against that. I'm glad I did, because that moment of pride could have cost me my life.

Pride Before the Fall
When Denial Turns Dangerous

I won't live to see thirty—yeah, right. I can't believe she said that to me. Doctors are so dramatic. That's what I kept telling myself after the visit. Those six words continued to replay in my mind, over and over. At twenty-six, I had a hard time processing my emotions about it— my fear was moonlighting as anger and irritation. But just like everything else regarding my health, I eventually went numb over it. "Welp, I'm going to die at thirty," I would tell my family. I was trying to make light of the situation, using jokes to mask my real concerns and fears. But deep down, my father and his health were heavy on my mind. Once again, I convinced myself that I had fourteen more years before any of that happened.

But it brought me back to the reality I had been avoiding: my health. I reflected on my actions and lifestyle. I considered my cholesterol and how poorly I was managing it, especially regarding my diet. I didn't want to return to any medical professionals to hear things I already knew—like which foods to eat or the importance of exercising. However, I *thought* about getting serious. I couldn't run from this forever, and even though I believed my issues wouldn't surface until my forties, my goal was still to outlive my father. I didn't want to die, but I wasn't helping myself. I believed I knew all I needed to in order to do better, but I was more ignorant about the subject than I realized, which gave me a false sense of what it means to be healthy.

In my journey to get healthier, the only thing I managed to do was follow up with the lipid specialist at the Ohio State Medical Center. I surprised myself by going, especially after my last visit. I was already at odds with the doctors, but in this instance, the good side of my conscience prevailed and convinced me to go. A lipid specialist diagnoses, manages, and treats disorders related to lipids, including cholesterol and triglycerides. They possess expert knowledge on addressing lipid issues, particularly those that may lead to cardiovascular problems. They help patients identify and avoid risk factors.

During the visit, the doctor reiterated the concerns expressed by the first doctor. However, she had a better delivery, which makes sense. As a lipid specialist, she may have seen young people with cholesterol as high as mine. We reviewed various options, which included medication and an ultrasound. We started with medicine to lower my cholesterol. I finally gave in and took the medicine to help control my condition. The ultrasounds were to look inside my heart and neck to see if I had plaque buildup. The only catch was that my insurance company would not cover it. That was new for me. As mentioned, my insurance covered everything, with minimal out-of-pocket expenses. However, on that day, I encountered an exception.

Before the doctor got to the cost, she explained that I would have to come in for two sessions. One would be a detailed ultrasound of the carotid arteries in my neck to see if there were any blockages there and to assess my risk of a stroke. This is called a carotid ultrasound. Carotid arteries are crucial because they supply oxygen-rich blood to your brain. The second test was a standard echocardiogram, often referred to as an "echo," which is an ultrasound of the heart. It primarily focuses on the heart's structure and function. The doctors would check how my heart was pumping and how well it was working.

Each test serves as a vital tool that provides unique and important information about the cardiovascular system. Along with symptoms, risk factors, and overall health, these tests help your doctor gain a clearer understanding of your heart and blood vessel health, enabling them to determine the initial steps for treatment. However, these tests would have cost me three hundred dollars each, totaling six hundred dollars out of pocket. Believe it or not, six hundred dollars could have made the difference in preventing my heart attack.

But upon hearing about the cost, I had had enough. I just needed to do a better job and cut back on certain foods, and I would be all right, I thought. It was becoming too much for me. I wasn't mentally prepared to really deal with my health just yet, so I didn't want to go through all of this medical stuff. But that was my pride talking. Pride and denial wouldn't let me accept that I needed help. As Proverbs 16:18 says, "Pride goeth before destruction, and an haughty spirit before a fall" (KJV). Or, more commonly said:

"Pride comes before a fall."

When you put things into perspective, it's crazy that I didn't believe my life was worth six hundred dollars. I undervalued my existence, a misstep that I am thankful didn't cost me my life. However, this situation is more common than you might think. According to the Kaiser Family Foundation, "About one-third (36%) of adults say that in the past 12 months they have skipped or postponed getting the health care they needed because of the cost. Notably, three in four (75%) uninsured adults under age 65 say they went without needed care because of the cost."

Since I declined the follow-up test, I committed to at least taking my medication, but that didn't last long. I started taking a statin, which is a drug that lowers the level of LDL cholesterol in the blood. But when I ran out, I never went to refill my prescription. I thought I was still too young for those medications, and I didn't want to pay for them. Even though they were low-cost, I again didn't appreciate my life enough to follow through.

The truth is that life is priceless. No amount of money should keep you from saving or improving a life, especially your own. Unfortunately, health care is expensive and unaffordable for some. The Kaiser Family Foundation states, "The cost of prescription drugs prevents some people from filling prescriptions. About one in five adults (21%) say they have not filled a prescription because of the cost, while a similar share (23%) say they have instead opted for over-the-counter alternatives. About one in seven adults say they have cut pills in half or skipped doses of medicine in the last year because of the cost."

I had the money but didn't want to invest in myself. At twenty-six, I struggled to envision a life in which I had to take medicine every day. It felt too soon to follow the path my father took. Even though the pills weren't expensive, it was money that could be spent on other things. My excuses began to lead me back down a path of complacency regarding my health. I kept reminding myself that this was my life and that I had time to adjust my lifestyle. Moreover, I come from a praying family, echoing the same sentiments we expressed during my father's health battles. Once again, another hint at predicting my fate seemed to align with my father's in terms of our health.

But again, the goal was to outlive my father and not pass away in my fifties. So I began to recall all the things I believed were healthy in an effort to change my habits. I feel embarrassed even mentioning these changes that I thought were healthy, as it reveals my ignorance about what *healthy* truly means. For instance, I started ordering large meals, replacing my previous choices of supersize, biggie, and king-size meals. I experimented with different menu items, choosing fried chicken strips instead of burgers, assuming that since chicken is a leaner meat than beef, it would be better. This reminded me of my childhood days when my mom switched us to ground turkey and more chicken dishes. I tried to cook more at home and decided against using butter, as it is a cholesterol factor, and began using margarine.

Why margarine? The short answer is marketing. I started using margarine because, in my research, it seemed like the better option. Companies often market margarine as a cholesterol-free butter substitute, contributing to its widespread use. Researchers have also indicated that margarine contains higher amounts of monounsaturated and polyunsaturated fats (the good fats). Unsaturated fats help lower bad cholesterol in the body. However, I didn't conduct enough research because margarine is actually worse. Marketing misleads us. Terms like "zero fat" or "cholesterol-free" suggest they are good, but completely overlook how these products are made. While margarine is cholesterol-free, it contains trans fats (in this case, partially hydrogenated oils). Research has shown that these fats are worse than saturated fats because they increase your risk of cardiovascular disease.

I even developed a workout routine. As I mentioned earlier, by then, my days of playing pickup basketball and participating in flag football leagues were coming to an end. I didn't find time for much else between my jobs and social life. I was starting to develop a belly, which was a new experience for me, though I was still relatively small. My average weight was around 170 pounds, but I was creeping up to 185 and then 190, and it didn't look good.

But I got it together and found what worked for me. I started Shaun T's Insanity program. For ninety days, I did the program every single day. I didn't follow the diet plan, but I eliminated fried foods and pizza. It made a difference; I lost a few pounds and started feeling and looking good again. I was now more confident about working out with my friends. Exercising alone is one thing, but when I worked out with friends, I noticed something. While they recovered from the latest rep or set we had completed, I would still be gasping for air. Even after finishing the program, I still felt like I was out of shape, huffing, puffing, and gasping for breath. It was so noticeable that my friends questioned my fitness level. It was embarrassing, but it only motivated me to push harder. One small decision would ultimately save my life.

14

High-Five
The Highs of Life

There have been two times in my life when my breath was taken away. One was during my heart attack, when I couldn't gather enough air for a satisfying full breath, but that wasn't the first time. The first was back in June 2011. That was the day I first saw my queen, my best friend, my goddess, and my future wife—Alexis. Since I met her, Alexis has helped me become a better man. We've faced many ups and downs, trials and tribulations, but we've always overcome our challenges together. We both come from families with generational curses, and together we've decided to break them, live differently and freely, and create our own family traditions and vision. My life and relationship with her are the biggest reasons I fight to stay #HeartStrong. When I talk about protecting your heart and everything in it, she is the literal definition. Not only is she my biggest supporter and the love of my life, but she is also my heart in human form. And with God's timing, she arrived right on time to help me change my life, ultimately saving it. Even after all these years, I still remember meeting her for the first time as if it were yesterday.

It was Wednesday, June 1, 2011—an exciting day on the campus of Ohio State University. My fraternity, Alpha Phi Alpha, had returned after not having a presence on campus for years. This was a monumental moment for the university since the Alpha chapter at Ohio State holds historical significance. Established in 1911 as the Kappa Chapter, the tenth chapter in our fraternity's history, it carries a century of legacy. Typically, new members are introduced in a high-energy and entertaining manner. We refer to these introductions as "probate shows," and people from campus and around the city and state come to see who made the cut. The Alphas at Ohio State put on a show that day, making it clear to OSU's campus that they were back—and in a big way.

It was a cause for celebration, as Alpha brothers, friends, and family wanted to shower the new members with love and affection. The event was slightly earlier in the day, so an after-party allowed people to continue the celebration. The festivities took place at a popular bar in one of the entertainment districts near campus. The weather was perfect, and more people were out than usual. Upon arriving at the bar, I recognized all the familiar faces; events like this had started to become predictable—all the same faces and antics. But as I made my rounds, giving out daps and hugs while scanning the room and making my mental plan for the next person to greet, I saw Alexis, and I had to catch my breath immediately. Her beauty and vibe took me aback.

Alexis was wearing a black sundress, standing tall and pretty, minding her own business. She was, and still is, stunning. I immediately knew I needed to find an excuse to start a conversation.

Having worked in radio, I can easily talk to people, crack a joke, or introduce myself to spark a conversation, but this was different. I worried about what to say and wanted to make a good impression. Luckily, Alexis was standing with a friend, a woman I had known since childhood, so I saw it as an opportunity. But as I approached, my mind went blank. I greeted my friend, but when I turned to Alexis, the only natural thing my brain could produce was:

"High-five."

"Hell yeah," Alexis replied in a "Rock on!" voice. Her response gave me the impression that either she was silly like me or a very interesting person. After she answered, she smiled, and once I saw the sparkle in her eyes, I knew she would be special to me. I didn't know how then; we had to figure that out. But even in our early days of dating, Alexis always cared for and loved me—sometimes even more than I loved myself.

Throughout our journey, Alexis has taught me a lot. Alexis is a big reason I took cooking more seriously. While I thought I had the answers when it came to nutrition, she proved me wrong in a loving way. For the first time, I felt I wasn't being talked down to when managing my diet and health. Alexis took the time to explain the basics. Even if it was a stupid question, she would educate me in a gentle way and then giggle a bit. Alexis helped me reimagine everything I thought I knew. To this day, I know she arrived just in time, and her influence was enough to help me avoid a deadly demise. Without her assistance, the doctor might have been right about my not living to see thirty.

But we weren't saints. While Alexis helped me make healthier choices, we sometimes gave in to temptation, and when we did, we failed miserably. We were still kids—I was twenty-five, and she was twenty-three when we met, and we've been together since then. We were still accustomed to the addictive taste of fast and processed foods. Being young, our metabolisms were still on our side, shedding any excess fat we gained from eating those foods. Looking back at our adventures, we can hardly believe what and how we used to eat. For instance, our worst food failures came from our dates. We would attend the local Triple-A baseball games in Columbus for their Dime-A-Dog Nights, where hot dogs were sold for just ten cents each. We would also get the maximum amount possible per customer. The worst part is that we didn't share; we each ate ten hot dogs!

Or, even worse, during our first vacation together, we ate as if there were no tomorrow. We went on a three-day cruise to the Bahamas, our first cruise and our first time visiting another country. Everything felt new and exciting. The best part for Alexis and me was the unlimited food options. From buffets and Japanese steakhouse meals to late-night snacks, the options were endless. We repeatedly enjoyed breakfast and lunch buffets throughout the day, with snacks in between. There were twenty-four-hour stations serving pizza, burgers, chicken tenders, and desserts. Alexis and I even ordered room service just because we could. We enjoyed the luxuries of a cruise vacation. It felt like college again, but the food was much better, and the fun was nonstop.

Our favorite moment of gluttony was during a dinner on the cruise. Usually, cruises give you up to three three-course menu options. Alexis and I decided one night that we wanted all three. We started with twin lobster tails as our main dish for this three-course meal. However, we were curious about the rib tips. We ordered another round of twin lobster tails when you might have thought we were done. I will never forget how shocked the waiter was when we ordered another round of entrées, but we did, and we enjoyed every bite.

But those were memorable yet rare moments. Alexis didn't eat like I did. She was more focused and better understood food, calories, nutrition, and weight management. Alexis started early—her health journey began in middle school as she started changing her appearance. She vowed to never return to her middle-school size again. Since I've known her, she has handled it quickly and effectively whenever she's felt herself slipping. That was the first time I saw someone so focused and committed to fitness and nutrition. Seeing her commitment naturally inspired me to get better.

As Alexis educated me about nutrition, I remember having to come to terms with some heartbreaking realizations. The day Alexis told me the truth about soul food was like finding out Santa Claus wasn't real. To be clear, she still eats these foods, but she does so in moderation, and she taught me what moderation actually looks like, giving me a better understanding of what a proper diet is. At this point in my life, I had moved out on my own. I was living in my first apartment and growing tired of fast food. Since I was on the road so much, I wanted to start preparing my own meals again. As a bachelor, it was a struggle. The primary goal was not burn anything too badly. But as our relationship grew, I would cook for Alexis to show off my cooking skills. One thing I love about Alexis is that she is patient with me; there was a lot I needed to learn about cooking.

During the first lesson, I learned I didn't need to cook everything on high heat. No matter what, my setting was always high heat on the stove—everything was "well done." But through her patience, she taught me about different settings for the stove, preventing me from overcooking everything. Alexis also told me how much salt was actually in microwave dinners—I didn't need to add any more. I was used to salt, believing a dish wasn't seasoned unless I could taste it. Thankfully, she helped me see things from a different perspective.

I had been insecure about cooking for so long and didn't want to learn how to do it. I was confident in my tacos, chili, and spaghetti—that was all I needed. But Alexis stuck it out through my worst meals to help me improve. During this process, I discovered a love of and confidence in cooking. I appreciated her feedback and would strive to get better. She taught me the truth about changes I believed I was making for the better. Through repetition, things improved. Alexis's reaction changed from "Hmm, can I give you feedback?" to "Not bad, but can I show you how to improve this?" That approach was a love language for me, showing me that sometimes what you need is the right teacher. And sometimes, if it takes longer to learn how to cook, stick with it—because it's worth it in the long run for your budget and health.

Alexis and I spent more time in the kitchen preparing meals as my skills improved. Those moments brought us closer. I was finally reaching the point where the mission surpassed burned food. I was beginning to show off my skills to my family and friends. In fact, one of the best meals I ever made is loosely associated with one of the most traumatic situations I have ever dealt with—similar to the stress levels that my father and family endured. Once again, our family was tested, but this time it ushered in a new chapter.

15

Heartbreak

The Lows of Life

Death wasn't new to me, having experienced the loss of an immediate family member at a young age when my father died. While it's never easy, it can feel especially impossible to get over when it comes unexpectedly. There is no single way to handle grief, as everyone copes differently. When my father died, I found my peace. Since he had been ill for a while, I had had time to process and eventually accept his passing. However, with sudden death and unexpected tragedies, I learned firsthand how it can be not only heartbreaking but also lead you to a very low point in life, causing things to spiral out of control quickly.

It was 2009, and my life had been steady. My sister Jocelyn had been back in Ohio for two years. She had married her longtime college boyfriend, and by this time, they had been married for about five years—no kids, just dogs. Her husband worked at a university about an hour and a half from Columbus. She was the closest family member to me, in terms of distance. Whenever I needed a getaway, an authentic home-cooked meal, or to see family, I would hit the road to visit her. Jocelyn also had a house closer to Cleveland, a forty-five-minute drive away, which she commuted to daily. She had accomplished her goal of becoming an attorney and worked at a large firm in Cleveland. This house served her well, allowing her to be between the university and Cleveland. However, the commute began to wear on her, and she started considering Columbus as her next living situation, particularly with the idea of expanding her family by welcoming a baby. Jocelyn eventually transferred to her law firm's Columbus office, making Columbus her new home. She spent more time in her home near the university, driving back and forth to Columbus, getting to know the city better, and evaluating whether Columbus felt like a suitable place to start a family.

But this was difficult since she and her husband already had two mortgages. At one point, Jocelyn suggested we become roommates. For her, it was a way to reduce driving time between all the cities and houses, rather than taking on a new mortgage. For me, it was a kind offer at the time, especially given my situation. I was still working in radio and not making much money, so she offered to furnish the place with TVs, beds, couches, and anything else we would have needed. Knowing my sister, everything would have been top-of-the-line and only the best. Jocelyn didn't waste money but invested wisely in living comfortably and practically. During her pitch, she mentioned that she would only be at the apartment three days a week and would rarely be there on weekends. So, the place would have been all mine. But my pride wouldn't allow me to accept that. I viewed it as a handout and wanted to earn a place of my own *on* my own. Looking back, I should have taken the offer—another example of how pride has led to bad decisions.

Even though I declined the offer, Jocelyn eventually found a home in Columbus, just around the corner and within walking distance from my apartment. It was only a ten-minute walk to a higher-end area of town, and it felt perfect. At that moment, I didn't feel as lonely as before; her presence made living in Columbus more comfortable. While I had close friends in the city who I considered family, there was nothing quite like having my big sister so nearby. Now, if I needed it, I had a proper support system, and her presence brought a sense of security that I had been missing.

When Jocelyn got settled, her presence enhanced my experience in Columbus. I now had a place to enjoy home-cooked meals. Jocelyn would invite me out and introduce me to some finer aspects of life—high-end restaurants and dinners at her lawyer colleagues' homes, which featured exquisite layouts and options. I even got to tag along as the third wheel when she and her husband tried new places. For once, it was something other than fast food. Through her work at the law firm, she had connections to many influential people in the city and was invited to significant fundraisers and events that required a plus-one. Whenever her husband was busy, I was the first person she would call, allowing me to meet and get to know these influential people, including her colleagues, coworkers, clients, and future politicians.

With Jocelyn moving to Columbus, we grew even closer. We had been tight before, but this was on a whole new level. We spent much more time together, talked, and got to know each other as adults. Our relationship deepened, and I loved that Jocelyn didn't see me as her little brother but as the man I had become. Jocelyn would seek my opinion, listen to, and consider my advice. She was also there for my most challenging moments and helped me navigate difficult family situations. Jocelyn became a voice of reason for me. She knew me well and would counsel me to make the best decisions and not worry about what others thought. Jocelyn's guidance was insightful. She assisted me in the early days of my relationship with Alexis when Alexis and I were trying to figure out some things. There was trial and error. And when something was my fault, Jocelyn would always find the right words to say and suggest actions to make it right. Jocelyn was always right. Through this, Jocelyn became more than just my sister; she became my best friend, and our bond grew stronger every day.

After years of trying to conceive, Jocelyn and her husband finally got pregnant. She was thirty-four when she discovered the news. At that age, Jocelyn fell into the geriatric pregnancy age range. While our genetic high cholesterol skipped Jocelyn, she still faced medical issues. Jocelyn was diagnosed with multiple sclerosis in her early thirties. Although it wasn't severe at the time, she recognized its potential to worsen. She began planning for that, incorporating her diagnosis into her birth plan. Thinking ahead, Jocelyn started developing a strategy for what life would look like when her MS became too overwhelming. But sometimes it's not your health that's the issue—it's the situations life throws at you.

Around the fall of 2011, things quickly changed during her pregnancy, impacting all our lives. After thirty years in his industry, her husband was let go for the first time in his career. He did not take it well and exhibited all the emotions associated with the stages of grief. He wasn't the same man we had come to know over the last fifteen years. Usually a charming guy full of personality, he became quite cynical, making it challenging to be in his presence. His energy became negative, as he was overwhelmed with grief, anger, and disbelief at his termination. But he was family, and we did everything possible to support him and uplift his spirits. We didn't know that this would mean supporting him as he made the surprising decision to pursue a job 1,700 miles away from Ohio while his wife was pregnant.

He was offered a job across the country and was eager to accept it. He considered this an upgrade and wanted to show his former employer they had made a mistake in letting him go. This was a challenging moment for the family. Jocelyn felt alone and abandoned during this period. She was pregnant, had two dogs at home, and was working in a high-stress corporate lawyer position. So I had to step up. I was already quite involved, but I had to take it to the next level. I did everything I could to support my sister. From walking the dogs to looking after the house when she was away, I started doing all the little things to make her life and pregnancy easier.

During these moments, Jocelyn and I would talk about the birth of her baby and how I would be "such a cool uncle." These conversations made her smile and helped distract her from the things that were stressing her out. One apparent fact was that I would play a significant role in the child's life, and in subtle ways, Jocelyn wouldn't let me forget it. During this time, I was in the market for a new car. Jocelyn would only approve vehicles with child seat hooks in the back, constantly reminding me that I would be playing chauffeur to her child. They didn't know the baby's sex; they wanted to be surprised. So, I didn't know if I would have a nephew or a niece. But whatever it was, I would love that child like my own.

Even though I spent a lot of time with Jocelyn and Alexis, they had only met each other in passing and never officially interacted or spent time together. They knew each other because I would tell my sister all about Alexis. The relationship I was building with Alexis was promising, and Jocelyn wanted to officially meet her. Jocelyn would love meeting my girlfriends to share her opinion and approve—or disapprove, in some cases. I trusted her because she had never steered me wrong. As Jocelyn's due date approached, I knew it would be best to arrange this meeting before she gave birth.

The date was June 17, 2012. I was a nervous wreck that day. It was the first time I planned to showcase my cooking skills to my sister. Alexis calmed me down and reassured me that I had it under control and that things would be fine. I played it safe and cooked spaghetti for dinner.

This was one of the things I knew how to cook before I met Alexis, but she helped me improve my recipe through her guidance. I still had a heavy hand with salt, but I took it easy that day. Salt wasn't good for the baby, and I didn't want to do anything to disrupt Jocelyn's pregnancy. To be sure, I made my sister her own set of pasta noodles. I prepared wheat noodles for her while I cooked regular noodles for Alexis and me.

The night was perfect. Alexis and Jocelyn hit it off way better than I expected. Jocelyn opened up, laughed, cracked jokes, and had a good time. Alexis did the same. That was refreshing because they usually don't open up so quickly. But it was as if it had always been natural and they had known each other for years. We spent a few hours together as they continued to get to know one another. All I could do was sit back and smile at the interaction.

After Jocelyn left, Alexis started raving about how cool Jocelyn was. Alexis was excited that they had developed an instant connection. Before Alexis could even finish talking about Jocelyn, I got a text from Jocelyn that read, "I like her." That brought a big smile to my face. Alexis had passed the test with flying colors, and Jocelyn wasn't a simple test to pass. In our text exchange, Jocelyn and I had planned to debrief about dinner with Alexis. Jocelyn knew I liked Alexis, and now that I knew Jocelyn liked her, too, I was excited and looking forward to the conversation. But unfortunately,

that would be the last time Jocelyn and I spoke to each other.

I already knew it would be a busy week for Jocelyn because her husband was coming back to town. By this time, he had been gone for about six months for his new job. Although he came back and forth to support Jocelyn during her pregnancy, their energy felt different. Even the family sensed it. You could tell they needed to talk, but the priority was a healthy birth first.

Shortly into the new week, I received a call from her husband. Although we were nearing their due date, we still had two to three weeks left. Still, I assumed the call was either about a favor that needed to be done or something related to the pregnancy. Instead, it was about her being admitted to the hospital. She had had a severe headache and went to get checked out. Upon examination, the doctors discovered that her blood pressure was extremely high, high enough to be considered a medical emergency.

With factors such as her age and health history, a doctor on staff decided that it was best for the baby to be delivered at that moment. A headache turned into an emergency C-section. It was a scary moment, but the doctor on staff assured us that everything was successful and that she would be okay. However, when I arrived at the hospital, Jocelyn was battling preeclampsia, which put her in a coma-like sleeping state. No one was worried at the time because preeclampsia is relatively common in pregnant women. According to Johns Hopkins Medicine, it affects 5–8 percent of pregnancies in the United States. I expected her to recover fully; I even remember joking with her while she slept about being back in the hospital, congratulating her on having her baby. I told her I loved her and that she should get some rest. The doctor told me she could hear me, so I made sure I was as positive and loving as possible. Since our father's death, I had kept it together and stayed strong in these situations. My sister and I had been in hospital rooms before for severe conditions, and we always had each other's backs. This time was no different.

My sister gave birth to a healthy, beautiful baby girl. The family couldn't wait for Jocelyn to wake up to meet her baby and become the mother she had always dreamed of. But sometimes, things don't go as planned. Shortly after that visit, I received another call. This one was more concerning because the preeclampsia my sister was dealing with had turned into eclampsia. Eclampsia is more severe. It can lead to blood clots, stroke, coma, heart failure, premature birth, and maternal and fetal death. Usually, when women with preeclampsia deliver their babies, it helps clear up the condition. However, since Jocelyn had already given birth, she had a very steep hill to climb in her recovery. The next four days were rough. Things got so bad that my mother and Shena came down from Cleveland. Jocelyn was still in a coma and had suffered from multiple seizures. She even coded a few times. Coding is when a patient is experiencing a medical emergency, most commonly a cardiac arrest, requiring immediate life-saving interventions. Every time she coded, her condition worsened. Every time she was resuscitated, it did damage internally. It was said that even if she made it out of the hospital, she might be in a vegetative state and brain-dead.

On the fourth night of Jocelyn being in the hospital, I received another call from her husband. It was 4 a.m., but I had been close to my phone due to this situation. I could tell he had been crying. He said that at that point, bringing Jocelyn back each time she coded seemed to be doing more harm than good. He made the difficult decision to let her go if she coded again, and he said I should get up to the hospital to say my goodbyes. Even though I arrived as fast as possible, it was still too late. When I made it to the hospital, I was greeted by grieving family members and a lifeless Jocelyn lying on the bed.

On June 25, 2012, my sister Jocelyn, who was only thirty-five years young, passed away. She never got to meet her baby girl or be the mother she dreamed of being. She never got to watch her daughter grow and guide her as she made her own decisions and became her own woman. Jocelyn never achieved her career goals or had the chance to establish her legacy in the legal field. It all ended—and quickly at that. One minute, I was introducing her to my girlfriend, and in the same week, my family was making funeral arrangements.

Jocelyn was the anchor of our family who understood the importance of traditions and the need for change. She could always convince me to attend family functions, even when I was reluctant to do so. Her death not only changed the family dynamic but also our world as we knew it. The loss of her guidance and understanding was deeply felt. Now I had to be the anchor for the family, especially during this time. I did my best to keep it together for the sake of my family—to be strong and the one to lean on when my mother and sister needed it. My mother lost her husband and a child. My sister Shena and I lost a father and a sister. It was a lot to deal with. But as strong as I tried to be for my family, I was hurting.

This hit me harder than my father's death.

I was trying to be as normal as possible, telling myself that death is a part of life, and, unfortunately, this time it came sooner than expected. But in reality, I had a hard time processing her death and turned to distractions to help me cope. Distractions ranged from overworking to partying and even drinking more than usual. I was slowly starting to indulge in things that helped me escape from my feelings and numb the pain. With Jocelyn's death, I learned how long the grieving process can be. My father's death was a lengthy process; he was sick for some time, which allowed us to better come to terms with his passing. But with Jocelyn, it was all so quick.

Initially, the funeral arrangement process and settling the estate served as distractions from the grief. We were showered with thoughts, prayers, food, calls, and visits. By entertaining so many people, we didn't have time to let her death sink in. We had so many conversations about her, it felt like she was still alive. However, when all that stopped, the grief and sadness grew. With Jocelyn gone, I felt lonely again. The emptiness from her passing, combined with my grief, led me to make out-of-character decisions that became my distractions.

I began to binge on fast food and processed foods once more because cooking made me think about my sister. I started to stay out later than usual because being around people kept my mind off Jocelyn. I became the one who shut down a party; I would be the last one to leave and was sure to finish my drinks before I did. At times, being out that late and drinking that much put me in dangerous situations and put my health at risk. But that was okay, as long as I didn't have to think about my sister.

With traumatic experiences, many of us turn to vices to cope. While vices can vary from person to person, some of the most common are overeating, excessive drinking, or giving in to sexual desires—all as ways to repress strong emotions. Even in processing my sister's death, I began to think about my father more often. I wondered if I was living a life similar to his and having the same reaction he did when he was stressed. I asked if I was headed down the same path as my father. Was this another genetic trait that I was inheriting from my father? I struggled with the thought of it. However, through that reflection, I started to empathize with what he must have been experiencing. I could finally feel the weight of the stress he carried during the situation with him and my mother. Those thoughts helped me heal and let go of any resentment I held against him.

I experienced a hurricane of emotions each day, but I managed to keep it together. For the most part, I came off as the same Sam. However, my actions and energy were telling the truth for those who truly knew me, even though I may have been telling a lie. I was in a dark place, and although I was too prideful to admit it, I believed that simply moving along with life would help me overcome it; my friends recognized that I wasn't right, even more than I did.

The person who got to know me best saw right through my act. Alexis was the one who brought me back to reality. She had a front-row seat during my grieving period and could tell I wasn't right, even when I smiled in public. Even when I didn't want to admit it, she saw my pain—my breakdowns and my raw emotional response to sudden death. One thing I will never forget is how she put her mourning aside to help me deal with my own. Alexis had lost her mother a couple of years before I lost my sister. Her mother's death date is a couple of days after Jocelyn's. Even while mourning quietly for her mother, she was there to support me and the rest of my family.

It was a tough time for us, and we bonded through it. We talked about our experiences with death and how we coped with it. It was the first time I opened up to anyone about how death made me feel. Things got bad for me, but they could have been worse. Alexis helped me get through that period in life with patience, love, and the ability to be vulnerable. She made me realize how important it is to talk to someone and to have a support system. It can be a friend, family member, religious leader, or licensed professional. Having the right person to talk to can make a difference and potentially save you from your path of destruction.

I am not in the same place I was before. Alexis, family, and friends pulled me out of that dark place. I've learned to put my pride aside and lean on my village to survive. I have even sought professional help to fully process not only the death of my sister but also the death of my father. The biggest lesson I've learned from this experience is that no one should ever feel alone; by seeking help and a healthy outlet, you can help save yourself from a dangerous spiral.

Jocelyn's death showed me how death creates a ripple effect deeply felt by those left behind. Our family dynamic shifted—Jocelyn had been the one getting everyone together, helping Shena and me navigate Dad's old issues, and serving as our voice of reason. Now, since I didn't travel to Cleveland as often as Jocelyn had, most of Mom's daily check-ins and outings fell to Shena. The transition was tough—we made it work, but I'd be lying if I said we don't still feel her absence every day.

The most significant area where we feel her loss comes with our relationship with Jocelyn's daughter—my mother's only granddaughter, and Shena's and my only niece. Thankfully, my niece is well, healthy, and growing quickly. However, we don't have the bond that we thought we would have with her. Before my niece was born, Jocelyn, Shena, and I would often talk about how we would raise her, the memories we would create, and the traditions we would pass down to her. Traditions like the trips to Alabama, which we endured as a rite of passage into the family. Even though we had started to fly down to Alabama to visit family, we would laugh at the thought of subjecting her to the twelve-hour car ride with snacks in the back as we drove into the unbearable Southern heat. We had planned to create new traditions at "MaMa's house." *MaMa* is what my mother requested to be called as she prepared for the birth of her first grandchild. But things didn't go that way.

Emotional intensity shifted between Jocelyn's former husband and the rest of the family. We had been spoiled while Jocelyn was alive, as she had always made family visits to Mom's house mandatory. We thought that would continue after she passed, but it started to fade away after a few years. A year after Jocelyn's death, her former husband remarried and started a new life far away from us, leaving us to hold on to the memory of Jocelyn while trying to build a long-distance relationship with her daughter. Unsettled emotions—primarily due to his decision to move so far away while Jocelyn was pregnant—mixed with our fresh grief. It created a storm of conflict between our family and his new life as we tried to navigate the distance. The truth is, we all needed to heal, and we still need to figure out how to do it together to create a new family dynamic. It's what Jocelyn would have wanted, so hopefully one day we will fulfill that wish.

Although we rarely see my niece, we do speak with her on special occasions. She is growing up to be just like her mom—intelligent, athletic, and a beautiful young woman. We just hope that one day we will be reunited and can tell her all about her amazing mother and our family. And while it isn't quite what we imagined in raising her, we will always be family.

Homecoming

Coming Home Again

After the loss of my sister, Columbus felt different. I tried to resume life as usual, but there was always a void, a piece missing. The family was still coming to terms with her passing, while her former husband had to move forward and focus on raising their daughter. His quick remarriage added another layer of pain to our grieving process. But we carried on, finding strength in each other and the memories of Jocelyn.

With my sister gone, I became more open to opportunities outside Columbus. That had always been a thought since I knew I wanted to advance my radio career, and the only way to really do that was to leave Columbus. I applied to various positions in cities like Houston, Raleigh, Detroit, and Atlanta. I didn't care where I went as long as it was a full-time job in radio. While I started out applying for promotions and on-air positions, I eventually expanded to different roles in radio—anything but sales, I told myself. But as we all know, God can laugh at our plans and has a sense of humor of his own.

In the fall of 2013, I received a call from Tim, a trusted coworker at the radio station, who asked me to consider a position that had become available. It was an integrated marketing manager role. I had no idea what "integrated" meant, but the marketing part sold me. I had inquired about the position the year before, but the location had been a turnoff: Cleveland.

I had no real desire to return home when I first asked about the role. My next move was supposed to be out of Ohio. To return to Cleveland felt like a step backward, and I didn't want to do that. Most of my friends were still in Columbus, and my childhood friends were scattered and busy with life. Plus, Alexis and I were growing closer, and her thoughts on the city mattered—she's also from Cleveland, just a mile from where I grew up, but we both agreed that outside of family, there wasn't much there for us.

But after a lot of thought and prayer, I decided to apply for and ultimately take the job. The plan was to get a full-time job, then look for another opportunity within the company or move out of Cleveland within two years. But in the meantime, my dream of working full-time at Radio One came true. Even though I never pictured that it would be in Cleveland, and even though it meant swallowing my pride, moving back home turned out to be the right decision. At least I wasn't the only one—LeBron James announced his own return home the same year I moved back, 2014.

This time, I was determined to have a different Cleveland experience. I wouldn't just go back to Warrensville or stick to my old circles. I wanted to explore new places, meet new people, and reset my expectations of the city. I chose to live on the west side, near the city's emerging areas, ready to discover a side of Cleveland I'd never known.

Moving west was a big step. Cleveland has this strange east-west divide—Warrensville, where I grew up, is on the east side, which is predominantly Black. The west side is more Puerto Rican, Dominican, and white, and it's where the newest and fastest developments are happening. Experiencing both sides gave me a new appreciation and love for the city. My whole perception changed—I wanted to show others that this was a new Cleveland.

With LeBron's return and big events coming like the Republican National Convention and all-star games, Cleveland was making a comeback. The city felt alive and exciting. I met so many new people, made new friendships, and deepened the old ones. Living twenty minutes away from everything, on a new side of town, made a world of difference. I was rarely home—always on the move, attending networking events and radio gigs, or socializing with friends. Rediscovering what Cleveland had to offer—the art scene, time by Lake Erie, our pro sports teams—opened my eyes to the fact that there was so much more than I'd ever realized. Best of all, I was there to witness the Cavaliers win the 2016 NBA Championship, Cleveland's first in ages—a peak homecoming moment.

When I wasn't in Cleveland, I made trips back to Columbus, since Alexis still lived there. Most of my close ties were in Columbus, so I visited almost every weekend—so much so that some people didn't even know I'd moved. I excitedly shared every new discovery in Cleveland with Alexis, hoping she'd start to rediscover her love for the city too. She wasn't fully sold and used to joke she'd only come back to Cleveland if I "put a ring on it." We were two years into our relationship and had more building to do before any decisions like that, so for the time being, my frequent trips worked for us.

Running back and forth meant less time at home to cook, and my health slid down the list of priorities. I dove into rediscovering Cleveland's food scene—the legendary "sauce on everything," classic pizza spots, Food Network–featured delis, and higher-end restaurants in areas I never explored as a kid. Living so close to downtown made it easy to try something new all the time. LeBron's return meant bar gatherings for Cavs games. My friends and I would catch games together—fried, greasy game-day foods and late-night eats were the norm. Trips back to Columbus meant fast food was the convenient choice, as always. We lived many nights like we were still in college, fueling up on late-night pizza and Waffle House. The healthy options weren't even on my radar.

Being home allowed me to spend more time on Sunday dinners with my family. Even though most meals were Southern classics—full of butter, salt, and fat—they were still better than takeout. Mom's cooking at least included a vegetable or two. Eventually, my lack of exercise and poor diet caught up with me again. Instead of facing it, I made excuses. I told myself it was normal for metabolism to slow down as I neared thirty and that being out of shape was just part of getting older. That rationalization was comfortable, but the warning in my head—the words of Mrs. Dunning and the doctors—was always present, quietly insisting, "Tick-tock, tick-tock."

I was twenty-eight, stubborn when it came to health. But my weight was creeping higher than ever, and my face grew rounder; friends commented on how puffy my cheeks were. "That's grown-man weight," I'd say, brushing them off. But that's a trap; we assume gaining weight is just what happens with age. While that's partly true, it shouldn't come from poor diet, lack of exercise, and overindulgence. But that was the road I was heading down—until an invitation to join a running club changed everything and, ultimately, saved my life.

17

Run with the Winners

I've always hated running, but I've always loved people. That love for people is what brought me to my first Saturday run with Run with the Winners. I accepted a casual invitation to a new running club started by one of my coworkers at the radio station. I had tried running before as a way to get in shape, but I never stuck with it. I thought running was difficult because it hurt my body, and every time I ran, it only made me feel more out of shape. But I couldn't pass up another chance to meet new people in Cleveland.

Run with the Winners—RWTW for short—is not your typical running group. There's no fear of being embarrassed or exposed for not being an elite runner; RWTW is an open, welcoming, positive environment where experienced and novice runners come together as one group. The club was started by my coworker, DJ Steph Floss, who was just getting into running himself. Floss is well known, so he often invites people along, and RWTW has even expanded to different cities, such as Toronto and Los Angeles.

The vibes that Steph created with the group made it easy for me to return week after week. I was finally finding a workout that worked for me. Before joining, I'd tried workout classes, but they didn't stick. I pulled out my bike for a few miles here and there, but it wasn't consistent. I even hired a trainer—a fraternity brother and friend—but unfortunately, he had to move out of town for work, so once again, I was on my own, still searching for a routine I could maintain.

That brings us back to my invitation to RWTW. Early on, my weekends were mostly free in the mornings, so I had no excuse not to go. I often turned down workout invitations because of insecurities. I didn't want anyone to judge me for being out of shape or see me quit in front of others. I preferred working out on my own, suffering in silence. I couldn't see it then, but now I realize those were just excuses and intrusive thoughts holding me back. This time, though, it was my radio family that made me feel more comfortable.

One Saturday, I finally showed up. I was nervous, having not run in years. It was a two-mile route at Edgewater Park, a large park right on Lake Erie. It's a great place to run: lots of space, beautiful water views, and nature all around. During introductions, I realized most of the group weren't experienced runners. The typical way to greet someone is to state your name, what part of town you're from, and how much you anticipated this run would hurt. Hearing others' fears about the run oddly gave me comfort, maybe because I knew I wasn't alone.

Once the run started, it quickly became clear who was modest and who was for real. For the seasoned runners, those two miles were just an appetizer—they'd finish in under fifteen minutes. The rest of us—the ones there for the vibes—crossed the finish line with distressed expressions, struggling to complete the run. That was me at first. My first run was a painful experience: chest burning, huffing and puffing long after, hands on my knees, gasping for air. Still, I wasn't the only one—most of us looked the same. What mattered was that we all finished.

With time, I began showing up every Saturday. RWTW provided the atmosphere I'd been seeking: no winners or losers, no first or last place.

Just the fact that you showed up was a win in itself. The experienced runners even started to share tips and encouragement with newcomers. Whenever a new face joined, we'd make them feel part of the group immediately. My love for people had never helped me love running before—but new friendships and a sense of family quickly overshadowed that. Many of the friends I made remain close to this day. The running group evolved into a genuine community, bonding even outside of run days and supporting each other in all aspects of life.

I attended runs so frequently that I started looking forward to seeing my fellow runners. I began buying into the idea of being a "real" runner: got the shoes, the gear, even signed up for racing events. Running wasn't just seasonal—I'd do it in the winter when bearable or inside if it wasn't. Running became my primary workout.

By spring 2015, I was a regular. I still didn't enjoy running, but I pushed through enough to stay competitive in our monthly mile challenges. We tracked our runs and mileage on the Nike Run Club app; keeping an eye on the leaderboard motivated me to run independently as well. I went from two days a week with the group to at least four days a week on my own. My goal was to run at least two miles, something I could do consistently to keep myself in shape. I could do it anywhere; when visiting Columbus to see Alexis or even traveling on vacation or during holidays, I logged miles. I was committed to being close to the top. Some runners put up seventy miles a month or more; I usually hit twenty to thirty. I realized if I stayed consistent, I'd always be near the top—and that's where I usually was.

As the group grew, so did our running schedule. Before long, we were running on both Saturdays and Wednesdays, challenging each other and even creating friendly rivalries within the group. The competition wasn't too serious, but it gave us extra motivation to push harder and earn bragging rights. Really, the bragging and rivalry were just a system of encouragement, fueling our progress and helping us reach new heights.

Running became the best way for me to get in shape, and I didn't want to let the group down. Why? Because I love people, and now they had become my people. Yet even with all the running, love, and support, I still felt like I wasn't where I wanted to be in terms of fitness. I could see myself getting faster, shedding weight, and feeling less out of shape than I had at first. But I still struggled to catch my breath as quickly as others. *Just go harder*, I'd tell myself. Fortunately, my negative, intrusive thoughts had gradually turned to motivational ones after I became a regular runner. But since I wanted to believe all I needed was to push harder, I ignored my body's signals—the ones telling me my body couldn't breathe the way it should. One day, right before my thirtieth birthday, I learned the problem the hard way.

18

I Almost Didn't Live to See Thirty
The Final Warning

Among all the warnings I received, there is one I rarely discuss, and that is the most unique. It was as if God himself were trying to get my attention in a new way. It came to me through a dream—not my own but from a person I have never actually met. Her name is Viv. She didn't live in the city, but she is a member of another Greek organization with which my fraternity shares a close bond. We both were part of a group chat between our organizations, a space where we could stay in touch and share experiences, even with those we had never met face-to-face.

Viv always seemed optimistic based on our group chat interactions. She is known for being kind, positive, and having an overall good vibe. I kept that in mind the day she sent me a DM asking for my phone number. She said she needed to talk to me because she had a dream about me and felt it in her spirit to share it. Hearing that creeped me out a bit, but because my fraternity brothers spoke highly of her, it allowed me to let my guard down and trust her. The fact that she, a stranger, had a dream about me was unsettling, to say the least. I gave her my number, and we scheduled a call.

Viv sounded just as I imagined. You could hear her smile and feel her warm energy through the phone. I needed that for what she told me next. She said she has a gift from God that comes through dreams. She doesn't get them often, but when she does, they feel realistic, and she receives them as messages. She acknowledged we hadn't met in person and that the DM could have seemed odd. But she was convinced the dream about me was so powerful that she was obligated by God to share it.

She told me that in her dream, she was at a funeral where everyone was sad and mourning a death. Initially, she felt confused, but as she approached the casket, she realized it was me inside. It's almost unbelievable that she would see me since she had only seen pictures of me before. While the grieving crowd thought I was dead, she was the only one who noticed I was alive, fighting through something only she could see. She urged the crowd to focus and see what she saw. She said she became hysterical and burst into tears—not out of mourning but because she was the only one who could recognize I was still alive and needed help.

She told me the dream affected her deeply; she couldn't shake the feeling that I was in danger. She interpreted it as me confronting something in my life where others might think I was dead, but I would fight through it. I asked her questions to understand what the dream might mean, but we came up with nothing at the time. I had just moved back to Cleveland not too long prior; work was excellent, my relationship with Alexis was good, and the family was doing well. So it was just a dream. After our conversation, Viv thanked me for being open to listening, and her final advice was to focus on the positive aspects and benefits of the message. That conversation occurred in December 2014. Just seven months later, what I thought was a rough morning after a long night was Viv's dream beginning to come true.

What a night, and now I'm paying for it, I remember thinking during a routine Run with the Winners event that Saturday morning. The night before had been long. It had started earlier than usual, at 4 p.m., because it was Memorial Day weekend and our office had closed early on Friday. The Cleveland group chat, full of friends and socialites, already knew the plans, so it became a race to see who would arrive at the meeting spot first. But before the fun started, I had to get my run in at Edgewater Park, only two miles from home. This had become my preferred place to run, and it was a common location for Run with the Winners. After the run, I went to a favorite local bar, which offered unbeatable happy hour prices. It reminded my friends and me of college and how cheap drinks used to be. Since it was a holiday weekend, the bar was packed.

The air was filled with good vibes, fun, and signs of a happy hour. It was starting to catch up to everyone since we had plenty to celebrate. The Cavs were making their first playoff appearance in years, and we decided to add to the excitement. It was fun all around. Alexis came up for the weekend to celebrate with us. After her two-hour drive, she was disappointed to see how deep I was into the celebration. I could see it on her face; she stuck by my side, a testament to the strength of her love. Knowing her, it was also to ensure I was—and would remain—safe, especially on a holiday weekend when excessive partying can lead to dire consequences.

It turned into an all-day affair. As more people arrived, the drinks flowed even more, especially whenever someone arrived who had come back home to Cleveland for the holiday. This added another layer of excitement and more drinks. We moved around to a couple of places but ended up at a house party. It felt like the drinks were endless. But that was fine; besides, it was a holiday. After 1 a.m., I'd had enough. My body was exhausted, I was hungry, and, most importantly, I needed to wake up early in the morning to run it all off with Run with the Winners.

I realized on the ride home why Alexis was upset. She was disappointed that I'd stayed out all day, putting myself at risk due to excessive drinking and lack of food. Drinking on an empty stomach never leads to a good situation, but I hadn't wanted to pull myself away from the fun. There was a time early on when Alexis cared about me more than I cared about myself. But I didn't see it that way and resented it when she did. Even when I knew she was right, I made excuses or found reasons why her concerns weren't valid. Alexis was right, but I made her feel wrong, and she dropped it.

When we woke in the morning, I did a "temperature check" with her to see if she was still mad. Thankfully, everything was fine, which eased my mind about the rest of the weekend and helped me prepare for the upcoming run. After a joke, a playful tickle, and a kiss, I left for the group run. That week's run was at Edgewater Park. Even though I'd been there the day before, I didn't mind. It was a warm day. We planned to follow an easy two-mile route, similar to the route I'd run a few days prior. The difference was that I was still feeling it from the night before.

Many familiar faces showed up, as well as some new ones. I chatted with a few regulars. We talked about the previous night, the good, the bad, and the hangovers. While we felt rough now, we all knew we'd still do all the things we'd regret throughout the holiday weekend. It didn't help that the group chat was waking up and already asking, "What's the move for tonight?" Usually, the group looked to me for the answer, eager for a repeat of the day before. But our run was about to start, and my only concern was completing it.

Steph explained the route and offered encouragement, as he always does. The group had become more organized after a couple of years, with experienced runners at the front to avoid having to pass slower runners. Intermediate and social runners started in a second wave. I was a social runner with some experience, so I paced slightly behind the experienced runners. For a guy who hated running, I had gotten good.

As a social runner, I would hold conversations with fellow runners, sharing encouragement and getting to know them while we paced and motivated each other. On this day, I needed it more than usual. We weren't far in before I was already pouring sweat. I felt heavier and slower than usual. Typically, after starting, the fatigue fades, but this time it didn't. It felt like I had to focus either on conversations or breathing because I couldn't do both. I chose breathing since a challenge was coming and I needed to be ready.

That challenge was Edgewater Hill, an eighty-eight-foot steep incline, like setting a treadmill to an incline of twelve. Even for someone who had run this route many times, it was a challenge. After the hill, the run would be nearly complete. *Ten more minutes,* I remember thinking as I started the hill. I always tried to attack it aggressively to get it over with, but I'd already used significant energy and was starting to struggle to catch my breath fully.

I broke pace and started to walk—rare for me. I always strive to keep running, even on the worst days. Walking meant something was wrong; I needed to catch my breath. But walking didn't help, and I needed to stop completely. Thoughts like *Why am I this tired?* ran through my head, but I thought I knew why: I was hungover and paying for it. Standing there with hands on my hips, gasping for air, I noticed the last wave of runners passing me. We were competitive, so that bothered me. It made me feel worse about the night before. Pride pushed me to start running again. Even though I hadn't fully recovered, I knew starting now might let me catch the end of the run and save face. As hard as I tried, I couldn't catch the others. Pouring sweat and gasping for air, I still thought I managed to play it cool.

But by now, my struggle was obvious, and other runners noticed. "Are you okay? Do you need some water?" a fellow runner asked. Her name was Tasha, and she was heavily involved with RWTW. On our runs, Tasha would stay back to ensure everyone was accounted for, sacrificing her own pace and conditioning to make sure no one was left behind—something I admired. She knew me well enough to see something was wrong. When I thought I was hiding my struggles, it showed all over my face.

Before answering, I had to admit defeat. Weirdly, I was okay with that—accepting my punishment. I slowed to a walk again. I wouldn't have asked for help if Tasha hadn't offered. Pride had always driven me to push through. But as Tasha waited with concern, I put pride aside, drenched and out of breath, and said, "Yeah, I do need some water." Accepting help shocked me, but I knew then something wasn't right—it wasn't the time to be tough.

As Tasha ran to get water, I walked further. My body was so tired; I still couldn't catch my breath. I was huffing and puffing, trying to get enough air, but it wasn't happening. I stepped off the running track onto the grass to shorten the route, but didn't get far. It was odd—never before had it felt this bad. After a few steps, I laid on the ground, hoping resting would ease the struggle. I felt like a football player who had been hurt on the field, needing medical attention. But while down, my thoughts grew louder. I felt insecure and embarrassed about being last, lying down, admitting defeat, and needing Tasha's help.

I looked and saw my car just feet away. I planned to get there, drive home, and tell everyone I was okay afterward. I didn't want to ruin the run or have others see me on the ground. Some knew about the night before, and I knew this would be a story I'd never live down.

Getting to the car and leaving was the only way to reclaim my power. My breathing had improved, although it was still not deep enough. I gathered strength, stood, and tried to head to the car. But my body wouldn't let me go any further. It felt like I'd just run a marathon.

I was the most fatigued and weak I'd ever been.

It wasn't smart to push myself too hard. Even after just a few steps, I started breathing heavily again, unable to get a full breath. No matter how much I tried, every breath felt quick, short, and unsatisfying. I longed for that euphoric inhale to calm me, but it didn't work. The only way to feel slightly better was to get back on the ground, so I did. Though out of breath, I now felt calm because my body was so tired. The ground felt as comfortable as a bed. It felt good to rest. Before settling, something told me to call Alexis. Without thinking, I rolled over to unlock my phone, which was lying nearby.

As it rang, I looked up at the sky—beautiful, calming, and peaceful. After three rings, Alexis answered, "Hello?" She said it more like a question than a greeting. She knew this call was unusual, especially since I was out on a run. The only words I could say were, "Hey, I don't know what's happening to me, but I think you should get up here right now." Her tone quickly changed to urgent: "Okay, okay," and she hurried out the door. It wasn't the timing of the call that concerned her as much as my asking for help that made her realize the seriousness of the situation.

I returned to admiring the sky, feeling peaceful, until a noise interrupted—a stampede. Annoyed, I turned my head to see Tasha and the whole running group rushing to me. The group treated it like an emergency. I don't know what Tasha told them, but they all came. Confused, I thought I was just resting, but to them, it was serious. Embarrassment crept in again; this would be a funny story later—stuck because I was hungover. For the second time that day, I couldn't hide my pain. I heard a woman say, "Oh my God, his pulse is low. Whatever you do, keep him awake." *My pulse is low?* I was shocked—and embarrassed again. They took off my shirt, fanned me, and poured water over me to keep me conscious. I was mad they took my shirt off—I've always been self-conscious about my body. Just then, Alexis arrived—oddly enough, she found me even though I hadn't told her where I was.

Two things brought me back to reality. First was, unsurprisingly, embarrassment—how to explain to Alexis that a stranger was rubbing my body. Second was the group's questions to keep me awake, like "Do you know where you are?" and "What's your name?" One question hit my pride: "What did you say your fraternity was again? Kappa?" a fellow Greek joked to lighten the mood. I looked him in the eye and said, "Absolutely not. A Phi A all day." Even in that state, I knew who I was.

After that, I began feeling better. Though I never got a satisfying breath, I was calmer and more conscious. The group realized I hadn't eaten or drunk anything that day—a huge no-no, though typical for me at that point in the day. Usually, I burned off the previous night's calories. Thinking that had caused fatigue, the group asked others in the park if they had food or water. A group picnicking nearby offered chia seed applesauce. Alexis saw it and knew I wouldn't like it. I'm a picky eater, but in that moment, I had no choice. She was right—it was one of the worst things I've ever tasted.

The awful taste immediately snapped me out of it. I told the group, "I'm good, thanks, no more." I had enough energy to stand and walk on my own. Things turned so quickly that some might have thought I was making it up. I accepted that this would be an embarrassing moment. I was a victim of the night before and just had to own it.

What I didn't know was that someone had called 911 while I was on the ground. Responders arrived after I'd recovered. I planned to tell them it was a misunderstanding, the result of a long night and nothing more. But my condition said otherwise. It was more serious than I wanted to admit.

Though I tried to avoid the ambulance, two things changed my mind. First was the fellow runner—a nurse—who took my pulse and gave instructions to keep me conscious. She was new to RWTW that day, related to one of our regular runners, though I had no idea who she was. It's amazing how God works in mysterious ways because this was the first time I'd noticed her with Alexis, the EMTs, and me. She provided the EMTs with a detailed account of what had happened and the vital signs that prompted action.

Second was Steph. After the nurse's recap, EMTs thought the situation was handled. They asked if I still wanted to get checked. I was leaning toward no, but Steph didn't think it wise. He had just run his first marathon and had his own medical scare, which made him urge me to get checked. Using colorful language wrapped in genuine care, he convinced me. Seeing what everyone else saw, I knew I needed help. To ease the group's fears and concerns, I went to the ambulance for a checkup. That marked the start of a day that changed my life forever.

19

A Memorial Day Miracle

As I waited at the hospital for the doctor to come in and give me an update, I glanced at the clock and noticed it was the time I had planned to arrive at my first BBQ of the day. I was starting to feel anxious, sensing that the process was moving too slowly and messing up my plans. At this point, I was in a full medical gown, attached to an IV drip, with support machines all around me and various wires and cords connected to my body. I even had a bubble wrap-type bracelet around my wrist. I had no idea what it did; all I knew was that it was uncomfortable and annoying. But none of that mattered as I thought, *Is all this necessary for a hangover? If so, it's enough to make me never drink again.*

Wondering how I had reached this point, I began replaying the day's events in my head, starting with the moment I entered the EMS truck. It began as a formality; overwhelmed by the attention, I just wanted to do whatever it took to get home. So, I attempted to show everyone I was okay and that this was merely one embarrassing moment. I didn't expect them to find anything because, in my mind, I was in pretty good shape.

I had sat on the stretcher in the truck, feeling impatient as I waited for the EMTs to run tests. With me were two male EMT workers. Alexis wasn't family yet, so she couldn't be in the truck with me as they closed the doors for privacy before hooking me up to the machines. I cracked jokes to lighten the mood and show that I was okay, a defensive mechanism to hide my true fear. But they fell on deaf ears, as the EMT workers were starting to get the results of my EKG test.

"Oh wow, we have to get you to the hospital; the EKG results are showing that you are having a heart attack."

You might think I would have started freaking out upon hearing this, fearing that the fate of my father had caught up to me sooner than I expected. But nope, that wasn't the case. Besides, the EMT communicated the news in a way that suggested *he* didn't even believe the results. It felt like the machine was malfunctioning because, on the outside, I looked fine. I felt much better than I had forty-five minutes earlier when I was on the ground, weak and fatigued.

Honestly, I didn't believe him because this wasn't how I thought a heart attack would feel. We hear the term "heart attack" all the time, but what does it mean, and how serious is it? While the nature of a heart attack is severe, it is often made light of. Phrases like, "Whew, you almost gave me a heart attack" are common responses upon hearing shocking news, as are claims of almost suffering a heart attack after a surprise or jump scare. Or most famously, comedy genius Redd Foxx on the '70s hit show *Sanford and Son* would have a heart attack in practically every episode, delivering the iconic lines, "Ooh... It's the big one... You hear that, Elizabeth?... I'm comin' to join you." He would clutch his chest and wobble as if in distress. It was hilarious, making light of a serious situation. So when the EMT told me I was having a heart attack, it was hard to believe.

While not all heart attacks are created equal in terms of symptoms, they all happen for the same reason. According to the American Heart Association, a heart attack occurs when blood flow to the heart muscle is reduced or blocked, leading to damage and potential death of heart tissue. During a heart attack, many people experience chest pain or discomfort that may feel like pressure, squeezing, or fullness. This pain can radiate to the left arm, jaw, neck, shoulder, or back. I didn't feel any of that, which made it harder to believe that I suffered from a heart attack.

Since I was skeptical, I didn't give their diagnosis a second thought or even give myself a chance to process it before I responded, "Listen, fellas, I had a long night last night. If you give me oxygen and an IV, trust me, I'll be just fine." The EMTs accepted my offer. Additionally, I think they wanted to rerun the test to confirm, as they didn't fully believe it due to my appearance. They handed me an oxygen mask and started me on an IV. This was my first time being on oxygen and an IV outside of the hospital. I have no idea why I requested it, but I'm glad I did. It was the first time I realized that the air we breathe every day is nothing compared to fresh oxygen. Indeed, it gave me a boost, and with the IV, I started to feel much better.

As I enjoyed the fresh oxygen and the satisfying feeling of the cold IV drip, the EMTs conducted another EKG test. To their surprise, they reported that everything came back 100 percent normal. Even I was taken aback. This further confirmed to me that I had just overdone it the night before. It seemed as if everything was fine with me, and I was close to being released. Before they could officially diagnose me as hungover, one of the EMTs asked, "Do you even want to still go to the hospital?" I felt like I didn't need it. I had gotten on the EMS truck and been checked out, so now the only thing left was to put this embarrassing moment behind me. Feeling like I was about to be released, I had to get my last joke off: "How much am I in the hole right now?" While it was a joke, I was also slightly serious. According to BetterCare, the average cost of an ambulance ride is $500 to $3,500 or more without insurance—an ambulance ride with insurance costs $250 to $1,500-plus on average, depending on your insurance plan and specific coverage. Although prices depend on factors like the location, distance traveled, and level of medical support provided, I knew premium oxygen wasn't free.

Jokes aside, the EMTs didn't want to risk the chance of the first EKG test being right and decided to take me to the hospital. They asked if I had a preference for a hospital since it didn't seem to be a life-threatening emergency, so there was no need to rush me to the closest hospital. I didn't have an answer since, at that time, I wasn't going to the doctor, so I wasn't attached to any medical system in the city. So the EMTs made the decision for me. It was my first time in an ambulance, and I found the ride amusing, from the sound of the siren to the flashing of the red lights. I was happy I was able to be in a state to remember it, versus their needing to attempt to save my life in the moment.

The EMTs took me to our county hospital, MetroHealth Medical Center. We call it Metro for short, and it has locations all over the city, but its main branch was about a thirteen-minute ride away. Upon arrival, the EMTs briefed the doctors on my situation, and they immediately rolled me back into an examination room. Alexis followed the ambulance to the hospital and was there to answer the follow-up questions the doctors had. As the doctors ran additional tests to understand what had happened, a hospital staff worker entered the room to ask questions. What I didn't know is that hospitals, including emergency rooms, are legally required to ask if you have an advance directive, which is a document outlining a person's wishes in the event they are no longer able to communicate on their own. So when I was asked about a living will, my immediate response was, "Am I about to die?" once again making light of the situation. The hospital worker smirked and assured me that it was just hospital protocol.

I was initially considered a curious case, as the doctors were just as confused as the EMTs were when they reviewed my results. However, after further examination, they uttered words that brought everything to a halt: "Sir, we think you had a heart attack." This was the second time I had heard that that day. Upon hearing it again, the jokes stopped, and reality started to set in. My mind began to race, and my first thoughts were about my father. *It's way too early for this*, I thought, as I had convinced myself for years that this wouldn't be an issue until I reached my forties. I was so convinced that my immediate response was,

"Yeah, right. I couldn't have had a heart attack; I'm only twenty-nine years old."

The doctors couldn't be sure without more tests, and they left the room to give me a moment before rolling me into the testing lab. The energy in the room shifted. For the first time that day, I was completely silent, trying to process the news and overcome my shock. Alexis was in the room with me and could tell that the news had affected me. Thoughts of my father and his health struggles were flooding my mind, along with worry that my struggles had started much earlier than expected and that my mortal life clock had started counting down. All of the thoughts in the moment overwhelmed me, and I broke down. I usually held back tears or strong emotions around Alexis because I never wanted to seem emotional in front of her. But at that moment, I couldn't hold it back. I didn't know what was going to happen next, but the moment reminded me I am human and I could die early just like my father. But the moment was brief, as I felt I had to get it together before the doctors came back in.

The doctors found an open lab and prepped me for testing. Before they took me back, I turned to Alexis and said, "Lex, don't call my mom." This was already becoming a stressful situation, and I didn't want my mother or my sister to have to relive another heart health emergency. Plus, I was hoping this was still a misunderstanding and just another chapter in the story of the worst hangover of my life. And if it was, I had no idea how I would explain that to my mother at all, and most importantly, I didn't want to disappoint her.

The doctors rolled me into an open catheterization laboratory, known as a cath lab for short. A cath lab is a specialized hospital room that employs imaging equipment to diagnose and treat heart conditions. I sat there for a while as the doctors rushed to find anyone available to assist with testing. Since it was a holiday weekend, it took some time, as they had to persuade doctors to stay after their shifts or come in from other departments to perform an angiography. During this procedure, doctors injected dye into my blood vessels to see them clearly and identify blockages, abnormalities, or other issues. It was quick, and the doctors didn't tell me what was going on or what they found. All they did was request more doctors, nurses, and specialists to come to the cath lab.

What I thought would be a quick, thirty-minute process began to feel much longer. The doctors started to prepare me for some type of invasive procedure, requiring them to go in through a major vein in either my leg or wrist. It became personal, as a nurse had to shave part of my pubic area as part of the preparation. It was odd because they only shaved one side of my pubic area. "Can you shave the other side and make it even?" I asked the nurse, again trying to lighten the mood and keep myself from being scared. However, my humor wasn't well-received; the nurse replied, "Sir, this isn't a joke," in a serious tone.

Fortunately, the doctors decided to perform the procedure through my wrist; otherwise, if they had gone through my groin, the recovery time would have been longer. I moved on to the next step: an angioplasty. This should not be confused with an angiography, as their names are similar but different. I couldn't see much of what was happening since the machine used to view my heart was so large it blocked my view, nor did I know what was happening. I had a clear view of my wrist and felt a slight pinch as the doctors began to insert a long wire into my wrist, winding through my blood vessels and heading directly for my heart. It struck me as odd that I wasn't put to sleep during the procedure, making me think it wasn't a "real" surgery. That's when I felt the catheter snake through my arteries and eventually reach my heart. It was a strange feeling to feel them inside my heart while awake, but I remained calm. I was lightly sedated and was being given nitroglycerin every fifteen minutes. Nitroglycerin is commonly used to treat and prevent angina, the medical term for chest pain.

During the procedure, the doctors didn't give me any news or details. That, along with being awake the entire time, made me think that I would be out of the hospital in time to enjoy the rest of the day and the Memorial Day weekend, which brings me back to the moment in the hospital room where I waited impatiently for the doctor's release. The bubble wrap on my wrist was from the doctor's going into my wrist for the procedure, but it didn't seem like enough reason to keep me in the hospital. However, things were indeed more serious than I had thought, and I was glad that Alexis had wisely defied my request and called my family after all.

The doctor came in to see me and had a look of shock and surprise on her face. Before the doctor could even speak, I asked, "So when am I getting out of here?" The doctor could tell I was anxious and that I didn't fully know what was going on.

"Sir, you're not going anywhere; you just had a massive heart attack."

The doctor continued with even more shocking news. There were two significant discoveries in the cath lab. The first was my cholesterol numbers. Doctors discovered my cholesterol level was 475—more than double the number it ought to be. My cholesterol was so high that my body had started to develop plaque buildup in my arteries, causing a 95 percent blockage in my right coronary artery (RCA) and a 15 percent blockage in another artery, reducing blood flow. While any blockage is concerning, the doctors were more worried about the blockage in the right coronary artery, as it supplies oxygen and nutrients to the right side of the heart. This is why the doctors sprang into action and performed the angioplasty to clear the blockages and placed a stent in my RCA to keep the artery open. The doctor then said, with a completely surprised tone,

"We don't know how you are alive."

The doctors looked at me as a miracle and emphasized that I was fortunate to still be alive after the massive heart attack I had suffered. After more questions and discovering that I frequently ran, they attributed my survival to my running activity. Since I was a runner, my body had become accustomed to forcing blood through my blockage. Upon hearing that, the issues I had been facing, such as struggling to recover after workouts and feeling severely out of breath, started to make sense. I was in shape, but I had an obstruction that was both a gift and a curse. It made me feel as if I couldn't get in shape and had to work harder. However, on the downside, it was preventing my body from getting adequate blood, nutrients, and oxygen to the right side of my heart, slowing my recovery.

But why that day and why during a workout? I was confused as I tried to process all this information because I thought that working out would have prevented those problems and kept them away. Not to mention, I ran frequently, so why hadn't this happened before? The answer wasn't a shock; it had been in front of me all along. While there were several factors, including skipping breakfast and not drinking water before the run, oddly enough, part of the reason it happened when it did was that I was hungover. I was dehydrated. Baptist Health tells us that when dehydrated, the body loses more fluids than it takes in, leading to a decrease in blood volume. As blood volume decreases, the concentration of blood components, such as red blood cells, proteins, and salts, increases. This makes the blood more viscous, or thick. My blood was so thick that my heart had to work overtime to force the blood through my blockage, and on the day of the heart attack, it finally reached its limit. That's why it's a good thing I listened to my body during the run, took breaks, and walked when I needed to. If I had kept pushing through that resistance, it likely would have led to cardiac arrest or immediate death.

The third time I was told I had a heart attack was the charm. Everything started to sink in, including how truly bad my health was, how being active had saved me, and that there would be no BBQs that day or weekend. As crazy as that thought may seem, it was because, even while sitting in a hospital bed after suffering a major heart attack, I felt like I was letting my friends down by being away from the action. These feelings were magnified when I finally got access to my phone and saw all the messages from the group chat, eager to relive the night before for round two.

But excitement turned into disbelief as Alexis announced to the group that I had suffered a heart attack. The group was stunned, scared, and confused. "Is this a joke?" one asked. Most had been out celebrating with me the day before, which made it harder for them to process how it had all happened so quickly. Before I knew it, my hospital room went from just family visiting to almost everyone I knew in the city. They brought Memorial Day to me, with visitors every thirty minutes. There was a nonstop rotation of love, laughs, good vibes, and prayers from extended family, childhood friends, and coworkers. At one point, my roommate asked, "Are you famous?" He couldn't believe all the people who were in and out to see me, some familiar faces and voices he recognized on TV and the radio. Even Tasha, who had initially helped me, came to visit, allowing me to truly thank her for saving my life—prompting me to call her my "guardian angel."

The visitors kept me in high spirits, but my release day on Monday couldn't come soon enough. While thankful that the doctors and nurses had saved my life, I was ready to go home. Before my release, doctors had to run final tests to see if I had any heart damage and how much. When the heart is deprived of oxygen for prolonged periods, the affected heart muscle dies or is severely damaged. The longer the blockage lasts, the greater the damage, including improper function and scar tissue development, which weakens the heart's pumping ability—key information for my treatment and recovery plan.

Sunday felt like the longest day ever, but Monday finally arrived. When I saw a nurse, I asked, "Excuse me, nurse, do you know when the doctor will be around to run the heart test?" The nurse checked my vitals and said, "Oh, there won't be a test today; everyone is out enjoying ribs and barbecue." Her answer annoyed me, as I realized I would have to stay another day, and it reminded me I couldn't have

BBQ. From the ambulance to then, I'd been focused solely on leaving the hospital, not on what had happened.

I almost died, and it could have all been prevented.

And I had had plenty of warnings, but I didn't listen. I asked myself why I was still alive, especially when the doctor had told me I wouldn't live to see thirty, as validated by the current doctor questioning how I was even alive. Memorial Day was quiet, as most visitors prepared for work the next day. Alexis had to return to Columbus for work. So, I had plenty of time on Memorial Day to reflect. I began to think about life on a deeper level: my life, family, friends, purpose, and legacy. It's sobering to imagine what your legacy will be when your time ends sooner than expected. But the visitors made me realize how many people care for and love me. It made me realize how much I take that for granted. Those thoughts gave me a new perspective on life and impact. It inspired me to inspire others and motivated me to take my health, wellness, and recovery seriously. The first step was showing the world how I would attack my cardiac recovery, bounce back, and start a movement.

20

The Birth of #HeartStrong

After leaving the hospital and adjusting to the new hardware in my chest, I started to more deeply process what had happened. In the moment, it had all been so quick, but now thoughts began to race through my mind, and the idea that running had saved my life was winning the race. It's funny how one small decision to be social turned into my saving grace. It also made me eager to get back to running. But I couldn't—not because a new stent was placed in my chest, but because a five-feet-zero, petite nurse with the energy of an NBA center blocked it from happening.

Obeying medical advice was a new thing for me. But it was the very reason I was introduced to Nurse Buddy. Nurse Buddy was the lead nurse for the cardiac recovery program at Metro. Cardiac recovery isn't mandatory, and knowing that made me consider skipping. Initially, I thought cardiac recovery was designed to encourage people who usually didn't work out to become more active. Since I was already active, I figured I didn't need all that. I was comfortable with running, and this heart attack was mainly because of my genetic issues.

While cardiac recovery is a comprehensive program that helps patients improve their cardiovascular health after a heart event, it also teaches survivors about healthy living, provides counseling to reduce stress, and promotes mental health. The program is designed to cater to individuals at different levels of physical fitness, from those who were not active before their heart event to those who, like me, were already active. It focuses on promoting physical activity to help people recover and get better after a heart attack, but it is more than just that. It's about making fundamental changes and showing people that a second chance at life is meaningful and worthwhile. The class met twice a week for ninety minutes over a twelve-week period.

My first day of class, other patients thought I was part of the medical staff until they learned that I, too, had suffered a heart attack just like them. I was the youngest in the class; the closest in age to me was about twenty years my senior. We usually worked out for an hour in class and spent the remaining thirty minutes on education. The workouts were challenging for me, not because they were difficult but because I had to go at a slow pace. While I easily forgot that I had a newly placed stent in my heart, I needed to build my strength back up.

As much as I wanted to push my cardio recovery aggressively, Nurse Buddy always stood her ground and stopped me from going too far. With her years of experience and guidance, she would remind me that this was a process, not an overnight transformation. Nurse Buddy had been at the hospital for what seemed like forever. She had rehabbed hundreds of people, from those in the best shape of their lives to those who were stubborn or didn't want to be there. But Nurse Buddy always had a way to connect with patients. With all her years of experience, she'd encountered multiple egos and hurt many feelings, which is why my nagging didn't affect her.

She always found the words to remind me that I needed to allow my body to adjust to the new stent, even when I thought I was feeling well. When I tried to sneak and increase the speed on the treadmill, I would hear Nurse Buddy burst out, "Nope, today you will be on the treadmill with a 2 percent incline and a speed of 2.5." I wanted to argue, but I didn't have the evidence or the knowledge to make my case, which is how I ended up in cardiac recovery in the first place. Nurse Buddy's role was not just to ensure my physical recovery but also to guide me in strengthening my weakest area: nutrition.

The educational part of cardiac recovery was truly eye-opening. For years, I had assumed I knew what to eat and what to avoid. But I never knew why. In cardiac recovery, I got those answers. We revisited topics such as food labels, and in class, we examined ingredients and their impact on the body. This knowledge was empowering and helped me understand what to eat more of and what to avoid. It was almost heartbreaking because I began to realize why so many of my favorite snacks and foods were detrimental. This emphasis on education in recovery made me realize the importance of knowledge in my healing process.

For instance, fried foods have always been a favorite of mine. However, things like French fries and other favorites, such as cookies, pies, doughnuts, frozen pizzas, and microwaved popcorn, all contain trans fats. According to the World Health Organization, trans fats are produced industrially by partially hydrogenating liquid oils, mostly vegetable oils, but they also occur naturally in meat and dairy from ruminant animals. Industrially produced trans fats are not part of a healthy diet and should be avoided.

Learning why trans fats are used was even more mind-blowing. They're mainly added to improve texture and shelf life. While there is a so-called FDA ban on partially hydrogenated oils, a significant source of industrially produced trans fats in foods, it's not as clear-cut as it sounds. Because of labeling rules, if a food contains less than 0.5 grams of trans fat per serving, it can be labeled as having "0 grams trans fat" on the nutrition facts label. This is commonly used as a marketing tool to make you think foods are safer than they are.

There are keywords you can look for to avoid falling for this deceitful tactic. If a label lists "partially hydrogenated oil," it means the product contains some trans fat, even if the amount is minimal. It's always best to choose foods with no trans fat whenever possible. Trans fats have detrimental effects on cholesterol levels, increasing the risk of heart disease and other health problems. Even small amounts are harmful. In fact, according to the WHO, countries representing almost half the world's population have enacted best-practice policies to eliminate artificial trans fat.

In the United States, the fight against trans fats has been a slow process. Only in 2006 did the FDA require the listing of trans fat content on food labels, allowing consumers to make more informed choices. In 2015, the FDA determined that partially hydrogenated oils, the main source of artificial trans fats, are no longer "generally recognized as safe" in food. This effectively banned their use in most foods, though with some exceptions and a phase-out period.

Cardiac recovery lasted for three months, from June to August 2015. For weeks, I left work early to go to class. While I protested, I never missed a class. Again, it wasn't mandatory, but it became crucial for me. I began to build relationships, immerse myself in the information, and, above all, develop a passion for health and wellness. Each week, I learned something new. It took me back to Mrs. Dunning's lessons on food labels, but now the information started making more sense. It's a shame that we often have to learn the hard way, but I was beginning to think of ways I could change that.

Nobody should go through what I went through, especially when it's avoidable.

That thought motivated me. Besides, my story started circulating on all my social media platforms. From Facebook to Instagram, people were shocked to hear about what had happened. The reactions were always the same: "He's so young," "He was active," "He looked fine when I saw him," or "He wasn't out of shape." It became clear to me that this is what people think leads to a heart attack: inactivity, appearance, and diet. While these are all factors, they are common myths and misconceptions. It's not uncommon for people, including some health care professionals, to judge health based on looks. But I became living proof that none of that is definitive. I had an authentic, firsthand experience to speak from.

Cardiac recovery was a revolving door of patients. Since it was on a rolling schedule, people would join the class, a couple would graduate, but most dropped out. After at least four no-shows, each of us knew someone had fallen behind. The hope was that they had learned enough to keep themselves safe. Every one of us had been through a heart attack, and none of us would wish it on anyone. Even as a survivor, there is always a slight fear of suffering another event in the future. But when you stick to the program, it prepares you to avoid those factors that could lead to a second heart event. It was full of tips on how to eat better, stay active, and prevent negative outcomes in everyday life, from the snacks you choose to the amount you enjoy. It's the definition of "controlling the controllables."

Celebrating a graduation was always special. Regardless of the time spent with the graduate, we knew that if they made it, they were truly committed. You could skip class at any time, but that only sets back your graduation. Completing a set number of hours was necessary to graduate. As a class, we made sure to celebrate every accomplishment. During graduation, Nurse Buddy and her team encouraged patients to speak. Most felt shy and kept their comments brief, usually just thanking Nurse Buddy and the staff and vowing to live better. I knew when it was my turn, I wanted to inspire my classmates with something they could carry with them after leaving the program. As time passed, Nurse Buddy finally allowed me to return to a comfortable running speed and resume running fully. With the education from cardiac recovery and time to adjust to the stent, I was in even better shape than before the heart attack. The more I learned in cardiac recovery, the more I began to apply its principles every day. Who knew I would learn so much in that program? It truly was life-saving.

Before I knew it, it was time for me to graduate. "Today is the last class for Sam as he graduates from cardiac recovery," said Nurse Buddy as she presented me with a certificate decorated with facts and favorites of mine. The certificate read, "I love running" and featured a picture of Shaun T, host of the Insanity series—a joke, since I'd told Nurse Buddy I was doing the Insanity program to get back into shape. A small sign to show the staff listened and cared. As much as I used to complain about cardiac recovery, it was a slightly sad moment. I wanted to give an impressive speech, but I never wrote one out. I had thoughts, but nothing formal. Yet, somehow, it all came together naturally:

Thank you, Nurse Buddy, for you and your staff and everything you have done for us these last few weeks. While I am ready to get back outside to run, I will miss all of you and the relationships we've built together. As most of us know, many don't get a second chance at this, so we are truly blessed. I have been reflecting on my life and this heart attack, the friends and family who have supported me, and how one small decision saved my life. All the love and encouragement I've received has become my motivation—and my challenge to all of you. Protect your heart and everything in it. What does that mean? Think about what you love and how much it means to you—your family, your hobbies, anything you're passionate about. Now imagine being gone and the impact that would have. From the family that counts on you to being the one who remembers the little things at the BBQ—without you, things change. So let those things fuel and motivate you to never give up on your health. Take a little longer to consider your decisions—making the right ones matters, whether it's parking farther away or getting in a workout on days you don't feel like it. Those are the things your body thanks you for. You're not surviving for yourself but for everything and everyone near and dear to your heart. That's what I call 'HeartStrong,' and I encourage you all to protect your heart and everything in it.

I received a standing ovation. The class and even the medical staff appreciated the message. What began as a speech grew into a mission, a movement, and a lifestyle.

While this saying came naturally and felt right, it echoes Proverbs 4:23 (KJV): "Keep thy heart with all diligence; for out of it are the issues of life." #HeartStrong's foundation—protecting what matters most. Which brings me back to my prophetic friend, Viv, the one who saw my heart attack coming months before in a dream. We lost touch for a bit, but after five months, we finally caught up. She was busy with her career, and I was adjusting to life as a survivor. We hadn't talked in so long; she didn't know about my heart attack, since she wasn't on social media, which is where most people learned about it. I knew I had to let her know, as I assumed her dream had been about this. We caught up, and before I told her details, I asked if she'd had any more dreams about me. Surprisingly, she said yes, but she wanted to hear my story first.

After I told her, she shared her second dream. I was nervous, since her last one had been so spot-on. She sensed my anxiety. "Good news," she said, which calmed my nerves. Then she shared: "Whatever it is you are working on, you're currently working with the intent to reach a limited number of people. In time, it will reach many across continents. Your heart will be overwhelmed with joy—not just happiness that passes, but joy from within, because you had no idea it would grow to this. And you will be alive to see it. It will be some time before you see it... It's already in the works."

What began as a speech grew into a mission. I coined "#HeartStrong" right there—born from that cardiac recovery room moment—and started using #HeartStrong on social media immediately after. To this day, the hashtag has inspired thousands who echo it back to me: "HeartStrong!" as they swapped fries for fruit, inaction for action, and delay for doctors' visits. People say, "Man, after hearing you speak, I went to the doctor," or "Your story made me start working out again." #HeartStrong has changed lives by showing that small steps protect what matters most. And hopefully, one day, that message will reach across continents—just as Viv predicted, and this time, I receive it with no worries, fears, or questions asked.

21

Protect Your Heart and Everything in It

Before we start this chapter, I have another exercise for you. Close your eyes for seven seconds. When you open them, what comes to mind? Was it a person or a passion? Whatever it was, it's important to you, especially if it was your first thought in such a short time. Now imagine never having the chance to see that person or do that thing you love again. To never spend time with that special person or share those memories that make life meaningful. Or to never watch a family member grow up and start their own family.

It hurts, doesn't it? Think about those moments when you achieved a goal that once seemed impossible or when someone relied on you because you're always dependable. Not being there for some of life's most important moments is a thought that people rarely consider. For me, the majority of the most significant moments of my life happened after my heart attack, a sobering thought reminding me that the best was yet to come — and I could have missed it all.

It was a gray, misty day on Saturday, May 21, 2016, two days shy of the first anniversary of my heart attack, once again Memorial Day weekend. Unlike the year before, when the weather was sunny and beautiful, this year the overcast skies threatened to spoil things. I had big plans to mark being a one-year survivor. Alexis didn't want to miss the day, as she knew this was a big deal for me. Over the past year, she had witnessed from afar how I had eagerly adopted the #Heart-Strong messaging, sharing my story with anyone who would listen in an attempt to raise awareness about health and wellness, showing people a real-life example of what happens when you don't take action. Alexis was proud that I wasn't all talk; I started to develop healthier habits and share cooking advice with others so that they, too, could be healthy. Most importantly, I joined the American Heart Association. It was important for me to support the mission of the AHA; learn the facts so I could underscore my #HeartStrong messaging with well-known and trusted, science-based sources; and be an inspiration and show people that, with proper management, genetic ailments are not death sentences.

We had a busy weekend planned, so Alexis came up earlier on Friday evening. We had an early morning start; fittingly, the first event was an American Heart Association event. From there, we would attend other events lined up for the day, but first, I wanted to go back to Edgewater Park, to the very same place I lay on the ground during my heart attack. I was trying to get my thoughts and words in order, as I'd been thinking all week about how to deliver a powerful message on such a monumental day for me. Alexis wasn't sure of all the plans that day; all she knew was that I had her undivided attention, support, and love.

"If you don't mind, I would like to go back to the place where I had my heart attack and say a couple of words before we go to our next stop. Can you record me?" I asked Alexis as we walked to the car after the AHA event. "Sure, babe," she said. She always loves it when I ask for help.

From the moment we got in the car, I had a flurry of emotions. Over-thinking my words while trying to remember the key points. Reflecting on the what-ifs, getting heavyhearted and even sad. Feeling especially sad that I could have missed this moment. I could have missed spending this time with Alexis.

The drive from the event to the park took about twenty-five minutes, and it was a silent ride. That was unusual for me. By then, Alexis and I had been together for nearly four years, so she knew me well. She knew I was thinking about something even if I said nothing. But she didn't ask; she figured it was a range of emotions from the day and wanted to respect that. Alexis was also quiet. I can imagine she also started to think about last year's events. I knew from time to time it would be on her mind, but she would quickly move on, as the possibility of my passing that day was a nightmare to her.

Either the twenty-five-minute drive was quicker than usual, or I was so deep in my thoughts that I didn't notice the time pass, making our arrival at Edgewater seem like it was only a few minutes. As Alexis and I approached the spot, my heart started to race even more. The feelings were intense, and I was extremely nervous. Alexis could tell—she felt nervous energy coming off me. Alexis thought it was the weight of the moment, and her calm nature helped calm me down. The plan was for Alexis to record my message to post on social media. I never really told her what I was going to say or what it was about. I had been preaching #HeartStrong so much that she assumed it would be something along those lines. She was right, but on this day, there would be more to it.

I started by thanking those who had supported me to that point and expressing my gratitude for being alive. Alexis had heard these words plenty of times. At that point, she could have told my story for me. But that's not why I was nervous. It wasn't because I was in the spot where I almost lost my life. I had been back a few times and even completed the run that I hadn't finished on the day of the event. I was nervous because I wanted to make sure I got the following words right:

"Alexis, in the place where I almost lost my heart, I want to offer you my heart for life."

As I said those words, I knelt on one knee and asked for Alexis's hand in marriage. Alexis was stunned. It took her a few seconds to process what was happening. "Wait, are you serious? Is this real?" Alexis is used to me being a jokester and thought this was a prank. Usually, with a moment as big as a proposal, family or friends might spill the beans or drop hints, or there'd be some elaborate setup to add to the moment, but there was none of that. This all completely caught her off guard. It was just the two of us, with no family or friends in sight. It was a special place and moment that I wanted only her and me to share. Besides, not many people knew about my plans, except for some family members and close friends, and, of course, I had asked her father for permission.

A few seconds of processing seemed like forever. I was already nervous, so now my thoughts turned to *What if she is about to say no?* To this day, I still joke with her that she was going to say no. It felt like I was down on one knee forever. "Yes, yes, oh my God, yes," Alexis finally responded excitedly.

The plan had never been to talk about my heart attack; it was to propose to Alexis. In the very spot where she could have been the last person I spoke to on Earth, I wanted to turn a place filled with negative memories and emotions into one filled with positive ones. This helped me mentally reclaim my experience in this place, preventing it from becoming a place that I would avoid due to reliving my trauma. A strong example of controlling the controllable. I was fueled by taking control of my story, by choosing love to replace the trauma and to create peace.

Our emotions during this moment were strong, symbolizing a new beginning and a reaffirmation of life and love. The thought of sharing a life with someone through different phases—the ups and downs, highs and lows, wins and losses—or rather, lessons—made us realize we wanted to do it together. Starting a family, growing old together, and having our family and close friends support us on this journey were all exciting thoughts near and dear to my heart. That's why I encourage people to "protect your heart and everything in it."

Why do people say such things as "with all my heart," "near and dear to my heart," or "a special place in my heart"? Ancient philosophers, such as Plato and Aristotle, believed that the heart is the seat of the soul and the source of strong emotions, including love, fear, and anger, as well as beliefs, memories, and hope for people who are deeply important or meaningful to us. This idea was reinforced by the heart's vital role in keeping us alive—its constant beating became a symbol of the enduring nature of deep feelings. Over time, the heart symbol evolved to visually represent these emotional and spiritual qualities, becoming an iconic symbol of love, compassion, and connection. So whenever someone says something "in their heart," they are expressing their deepest gratitude in the place where our deepest feelings reside, setting it apart from the mind, which is linked to logic and reason.

Being #HeartStrong is about protecting your heart and everything in it. It's about making those small decisions to protect yourself because you matter to the people you cherish. It makes your purpose in life to be present in every moment with the people and the things you love. This connection is at the heart of the #HeartStrong message, emphasizing the importance of our relationships and their impact on our health and well-being.

Austrian psychiatrist, neurologist, philosopher, and Holocaust survivor Viktor E. Frankl had these same thoughts. He once wrote in his famous book *Man's Search for Meaning,* "The more one forgets himself—by giving himself to a cause to serve or another person to love—the more human he is and the more he actualizes himself." *Man's Search for Meaning* is considered one of the most influential books in psychology and self-help literature. It has inspired millions with its message that meaning can be found in all forms of existence, even the most tragic, and that this search is essential to human well-being.

This brings us to controlling the controllables—a key part of the #HeartStrong movement. It's about doing everything you can to prevent unexpected death, including maintaining a healthy diet, exercising regularly, and taking care of your mental health. Thinking about others as a motivation for health reflects the idea that Frankl described. Making people and passion your purpose could save your life.

One of the most controllable controllables is diet. It is also the hardest. I knew that it would be challenging for me to make a complete one-eighty, like going vegan or just completely cutting out red meats or even fried foods. The truth is, I still enjoy all of those things. However, I had to learn what moderation truly means and how to practice it. I had to learn about balance and restraint. It doesn't happen overnight, but if you control your actions and get better each day, you eventually develop a resistance to these addictive foods.

It's not only about resisting but also controlling the types of food you consume, like increasing fruit and vegetable intake. Fruits and vegetables are rich in fiber, which helps regulate cholesterol levels. Along with exercise, they also help maintain a healthy weight, which is essential for heart health and supports cardiovascular well-being.

Managing your sleep is also essential. According to the National Institutes of Health, "Maintaining regular sleep patterns could help prevent heart disease just as physical activity, a healthy diet, and other lifestyle measures do." The NIH further explains, "It's unclear why irregular sleep patterns may have this effect. It may be partly due to disruptions in the body's natural sleep-wake cycles, known as circadian rhythms. Heart rate, blood pressure, and other cardiovascular functions follow circadian patterns."

These are only a few of the controllables over which we have power; there are many more. Minor changes are the key to unlocking better health. You don't have to make all these changes in one day, but as you incorporate more of them into your lifestyle, you'll see the difference, and your body will thank you. If I hadn't decided to run, I wouldn't have been able to experience one of the best moments of my life: my wedding.

On September 16, 2017, I gave my heart to the one who I knew would protect and care for it forever. Alexis and I got married, pledging our love through personal vows in front of more than two hundred friends and family from all over the country. Many people got to reconnect, make new friends, and create lasting memories. Some coworkers, family, and friends claim it is the best wedding they have ever attended. Many even have stories about paying for the fun by missing their flights the next day. All of it adds to the memories surrounding that magical day.

The wedding, or "A Cool Wedding," as we call it, was a reminder of why I started the #HeartStrong movement: love. There was the love embedded in marrying the love of my life, Alexis, and celebrating the beginning of our new life together. There was love from family, who traveled from all over to witness the special day. My niece, Jocelyn's daughter, was even a flower girl, bringing the memory and spirit of Jocelyn and others we have lost to be with us on that special day. We felt the love from friends, some of whom we have known a lifetime, like

Lamont, Nick, and J. Lee, who was my best man. And there was the love of new friends, like my guardian angel, Tasha.

The love from all those people was a reminder that I didn't owe it just to myself but to my community, my village, and my tribe to take care of myself and be there for them by making the right decisions, to be there for every moment worth celebrating. That has been, and will always be, the fuel for my #HeartStrong message—practicing what I preach and protecting my heart, and everything in it, always and forever.

22

Struggles and Setbacks

The year 2016 was shaping up to be one of the best of my life—until everything changed instantly. My career began to take off in January. I was getting the hang of the business side of radio as an integrated marketing manager while also holding on-air slots in both Columbus and Cleveland simultaneously. Alexis and I got engaged in May and started planning our wedding and future together. In June, one of the most memorable moments of my life was witnessing LeBron James and the Cleveland Cavaliers win the NBA championship, which as I mentioned earlier, brought Cleveland its first title in years and filled the city with joy. But in August, things got real—so real that my physical and mental health were threatened, bringing back stress I couldn't afford so soon after my heart attack, or ever.

Due to a freak accident, I ended up back in the hospital, but this time it was different. The stay was shorter, with no visitors, no jokes to lighten the mood or hide my fear, and—most importantly—this had nothing to do with my heart. Yet, this hospital visit triggered a period of depression. I lost my appetite, stopped eating, and dropped about twenty-five to thirty pounds. I lost interest in activities and stayed home more often. Being out and around people became difficult. I stopped working out, which, after a heart attack, was one of the worst things I could do. No more running, including Run with the Winners. I just couldn't do it. Eventually, I took a two-month medical leave from work. You're probably wondering how this all happened. Strangely enough, it all stemmed from one innocent moment—an attempt to relieve stress and have fun with friends—but it quickly turned into one of the worst injuries of my life.

Alexis and I met with friends at a local trampoline park on a hot summer day in August. We just wanted to have fun and feel like kids again. Nothing brings you back to childhood faster than a trampoline. But I was reminded that I wasn't a kid anymore. The park had a section for dunking balls, and I wanted to show Alexis and our friends what I could do—and prove to myself, as a thirty-year-old, that I still had it. As I built up momentum and jumped for the dunk, I felt and heard a loud pop in my knee and immediately collapsed. I realized I couldn't straighten my leg and knew right away I was injured. Because of the company's waiver, the staff gave me a wheelchair but didn't help otherwise. Fortunately, my friend Rachael, a nurse, checked me and confirmed that I had stable blood flow. At the hospital, I was told I'd suffered a torn patellar tendon, requiring surgery—always one of my worst fears.

The patellar tendon holds your knee together, stretching from the quadriceps to the shinbone and keeping the kneecap aligned. At first, I thought my kneecap was just dislocated; with no major pain unless I tried to straighten my leg, it seemed it could be popped back into place. But with the tendon detached, my knee couldn't move or bear weight, and any attempt to straighten it brought excruciating pain.

After I'd spent hours in the ER, a doctor finally saw me. I expected a quick fix, but instead he said, "Yeah, you're going to need surgery." I was devastated. *Not again*, I thought, especially after so recently recovering from my heart attack. But this time, it was even worse. Healing from the heart attack didn't force me to be completely down—it just slowed me a bit. With this, I was bedridden, unable to walk or move around, and faced months of rehab. Once again, I was sidelined just as I was getting back to running at full strength.

Resetting my knee was the first painful challenge I faced. Straightening it for the brace was pain like I'd never felt—even after two rounds of painkillers, it took five doctors and a nurse to hold me while they pushed the kneecap down and straightened my leg. I'll never forget that pain.

The healing process led me into depression. I couldn't leave the house; I relied on Alexis, my mother, and my sister for support; and the medicine left me drowsy. The forced isolation, pain, and medical leave created a perfect storm. Without physical activity to balance my diet, I started eating less, worried about gaining weight since I couldn't burn off the calories I was consuming. I was deeply worried—physical activity had been crucial for my health, and I expected to be sidelined for at least twelve weeks. It seemed like more than just a setback; it threatened everything I'd worked for.

But I had to regain control over my thoughts and empower myself not to let these setbacks define me. I kept telling myself, A setback is a setup for a comeback.

During that time, I realized that coming back from any setback is a process of its own—a real test of will. I had to accept what happened and focus on what I could control, rather than dwelling on what I could've done better. The doctors explained that my injury was a non-contact, clean tear—fatigued muscles, overuse, and a lack of stretching had made it almost inevitable. At first, I dwelled on the past, but I learned it's okay to feel angry, disappointed, or frustrated, as long as you don't let self-judgment take over. Acceptance and realignment of my focus became my fuel.

I channeled my energy into aggressively attacking physical therapy. Even when progress was slow and I started to compare my story to others' recovery stories online, I had to remind myself that comparison only steals my joy. Despite daily therapy, I was stuck at 45 degrees of flexion—far from what's needed to properly walk, run, or go up stairs. Everyone heals differently, but my therapist and I grew concerned. It turns out that collagen was a culprit—my genetic makeup led to excessive, tough scar tissue, making it harder to break through and regain my full range of motion.

Despite four days of PT a week and home exercises, I eventually needed a second surgery: manipulation under anesthesia to break the scar tissue. When that wasn't enough, the doctor performed a lateral release arthroscopy—cutting some tissue around the kneecap to improve motion. Even then, my range only improved to 70 degrees, which is still not enough to walk properly. My therapist worried I'd be left with a limp. I was afraid I wouldn't be able to walk down the aisle with Alexis for our wedding the following September.

Back at the doctor, frustrated and still not fully recovered, I received another X-ray and a second opinion from a professional baseball orthopedic specialist. He confidently prescribed a cortisone shot and set up a quick procedure. Again, stubborn scar tissue grew back within four weeks and required another manipulation under anesthesia. My therapist reassured me that high collagen levels meant I'd look young for years to come—but in healing, it was a real obstacle. Thankfully, after the third procedure, my range of motion and strength returned. I could walk, jog, and eventually run again. But it wasn't the same—concrete runs left my knee swollen, and I never regained my old distances. Fearing repeat injury, I turned to cycling instead, restoring my health and finding a new connection to my late father through our shared love of biking.

Throughout recovery, I learned about mental fortitude. Frustration, anger, and sadness were real, but I focused on embracing the moment and refusing to give up on #HeartStrong. Sharing my story online, I received encouragement from friends and strangers alike. It kept me going and reminded me that my struggle could inspire others. We all experience setbacks; they're a natural part of life. But they don't have to block your path toward your goals.

Acknowledge your feelings, but don't make a habit of living in that space. Learn from your situation; view losses as lessons. Focus on what you can control, and if you need help, don't hesitate to ask for it. Remember, being #HeartStrong is about those people in your heart—and if someone is in your heart, they'll be there for you in a heartbeat. Celebrate every small win because they build to major victories with enough patience and commitment.

23

What's the Move?

Rays of bright sunlight are usually the first thing that wakes Alexis and me on vacation. No alarm clocks or obligations to be anywhere—vacation is the perfect time for me to break away from routine and daily habits. Nothing beats being in a new, exotic place and embracing the people, culture, and food. Our rule on vacation is, "No worries." Work, extracurricular activities, and nonemergency family situations can all wait until we return. This is what life is all about for Alexis and me, and we wisely use this time together, creating unforgettable memories and experiences. From the drinks to the food, we indulge—but wisely.

Unlike the early days when we used to vacation, we have become wiser, especially when it comes to our eating habits. We've learned that just because it's there doesn't mean we need it. While we often reminisce about our cruise ship days, filled with multiple rounds of entrées and drinks loaded with sugar, we now know better, so we do better.

While we take a break from our daily lives and health-focused diets, the one thing we never skip is a workout. Working out has taken top priority after it was credited with saving my life during my heart attack. I want to emphasize that exercising and physical activity are a core pillar of #HeartStrong—by controlling the controllables. Developing a workout routine that you are comfortable with reduces risk factors such as elevated blood pressure, weight, blood sugar, inflammation, and, most importantly, cholesterol levels, which can lead to severe health conditions like a heart attack.

Now, I admit it—that doesn't mean Alexis, and I go to the gym in every city or even every day while on vacation. However, we do find ways to stay active and burn off some of the food and drinks. For instance, if we don't have access to a gym, we may walk several miles, skipping the ride to take in more of the city's sights. It serves as a good distraction; sometimes our lodging location could be a three-mile or more walk away from the sights.

Or if in nature, we may go hiking, being one with nature's beauty and bearing witness to God's finest creations. Whatever it is, Alexis and I make sure to stay active while on vacation, as it's crucial to our overall health and well-being. It keeps us looking and feeling good and helps us maintain clear minds.

As simple as it sounds to get out and move, it's not. Sometimes our mind tricks us into thinking that working out will hurt and is bad, preventing people from taking the first step. The thought of working out alone can be overwhelming for people. However, our thoughts are often worse than the actual action.

Once you start, not only will your body thank you, but it will look forward to your workouts. But it's crucial to ensure you are doing the proper exercise. If not, you will end up in another category of people who dread working out because they overexert themselves too soon.

This makes me think of the times I gathered the courage to start working out again before the heart attack. As I've mentioned, after college, I struggled to find a consistent routine. I was twenty-six and didn't have the same energy I had in my early twenties. Due to my job responsibilities at the university and radio station, I didn't have time for basketball and flag football leagues, so I decided to develop a new workout on my own. But I quickly realized I didn't have much experience. Outside of adult competitive leagues, I hadn't worked out properly since my senior year of high school. Back then, I was lifting heavy—bench presses, squats, deadlifts, and power cleans. That's all I knew, and I thought I could still do that in my late twenties. I was wrong.

I didn't realize that you lose what you don't use. I had lost a lot of muscle and forgot the proper form for some workouts. That led to wearing myself out quickly and soreness that lasted for days. My pride would kick in as I couldn't lift the weight I used to. Those thoughts, and how my body felt, made it easy for me to quit. Like most people, I thought that working out was supposed to be tough. I confused workout challenges with the difficulty of a workout. I figured that if I was tired after a workout, I did well, and I was getting stronger.

In reality, that's not the case. While workouts should challenge you, they shouldn't be so difficult that you don't want to return the next day. Knowing your limits and boundaries is key, as it helps with proper workout planning. The most significant factor is staying consistent, but it's impossible to be consistent without the right plan or when you burn out too quickly. Without a realistic plan, your workouts may be counterproductive or ineffective. So think S.M.A.R.T. about it.

In 1981, George T. Doran published a paper titled "There's a S.M.A.R.T. Way to Write Management's Goals and Objectives," which outlined the principles that form the basis of the framework. For over forty years, the S.M.A.R.T. goals framework has been a widely used tool that helps people set practical and achievable objectives. The acronym S.M.A.R.T. stands for specific, measurable, achievable, relevant, and timely. So let's think S.M.A.R.T. about working out.

Specific. Before starting any workout plan, ask yourself: What goal do I want to accomplish? When you set particular goals, addressing the who, what, where, when, and why helps you lay out a clear vision. It's important to identify because there are different workouts for different objectives.

Instead of setting a broad goal, such as "I want to get in shape," make it specific, such as "I want to lose eight pounds." This helps you focus on your goal and measure your progress. For instance, if your goal is to lose eight pounds, you could set a S.M.A.R.T. goal by saying, "I want to lose eight pounds in the next two months by following a balanced diet and exercising three times a week."

Measurable. You have to celebrate those small wins. Without progress, there is no motivation to continue. But first, you must set your timeline and manage your expectations.

Returning to losing weight, when do you want to lose eight pounds? In what time frame do you hope to accomplish this goal? Knowing your measurable steps helps you track your progress. If you plan to lose eight pounds in two months and after four weeks you've lost only two pounds, you can assess your progress, celebrate the small wins, or adjust your plan.

Achievable. This relates to people doing too much. Most set unrealistic expectations, setting themselves up for failure. This usually stems from bad advice, the misguided notion that you can do what others do, or a sense of pride. Back to the weight example. When considering whether losing eight pounds in two months is feasible, you must consider your surroundings, challenges, and traps.

Most people lay out their goals but don't consider the time and effort necessary. Or they forget about the little things. For instance, it's hard to lose weight if you're tempted by food, like going to a family member's house when they make your favorite dish or being at an all-expense-paid dinner where you can get whatever you want.

Those are the small-trap moments that could set you back. A smarter approach would be to set this goal when you can control your challenges. Remember, setting achievable goals isn't about setting the bar low; it's about setting yourself up for success.

Relevant. Losing eight pounds is great, but is weight the core issue contributing to the problem you're facing? For instance, for years the body mass index (BMI) scale was considered an effective tool for estimating body fat based on height and weight. But it wasn't created equally for different races and backgrounds.

It has been reported that the BMI scale, as traditionally used, has been inaccurate and potentially misleading for Black people, especially Black women, due to differences in body composition and the lack of diverse data in its development. Research shows that Black people, on average, tend to have higher muscle mass and lower body fat than white people at the same BMI. This means BMI may classify you as overweight or obese even if your body fat and health risks are lower than the BMI suggests.

People often think the BMI scale is a rule rather than just a guideline, which can complicate someone's weight loss goal. Knowing your body—what's safe, what's necessary, and what's essential—helps you develop a plan and identify if it is genuinely relevant to your life.

Timely. Finally, how much time are you giving yourself to complete this goal? Due dates and deadlines create a sense of urgency, helping you stay on track. After two months, you'll know if you lost those eight pounds and completed your goal. This is a good way to monitor how close you are to success.

Because one thing you can never cheat is time—especially when it's against you. So don't work against it; work with it. By thinking S.M.A

.R.T. about your workout goals, you're more likely to achieve them and stay consistent without burning out. Remember, there is always room for improvement. If you can't run that mile time you used to, don't worry; you will improve over time. Be patient as your body gets used to being physically active again. It's not how you start; it's how you finish. So be kind to yourself, and remember that progress is progress, no matter how small.

If you're not an athlete or accustomed to working out, try walking as a starter workout. While some people don't consider walking a significant routine, the benefits might surprise you. From enhanced weight management and joint health to improved cardiovascular health, walking does it all. It's not so much about heavy and hard workouts; it's about staying active and doing things your heart will thank you for.

If you are a person who needs extra motivation, don't worry, you're not alone. However, that's where technology can come in. To help myself get back into running, I used apps like Nike Run Club, which offers various programs and coaches to help you get and stay on track. And if you're interested in running but don't know where to start, try the Couch to 5K app, which is designed to get people without running experience ready for a 5K race in a matter of weeks.

I used these apps when getting back into running, as seeing my workouts laid out and receiving reminders really helped me stay on task. If you are a checklist person, these apps are definitely for you. They were a perfect way for me to build up to my goal of running at least two miles without stopping. Even today, I still use workout apps. I use Samsung Health to track all my workout activities, Strava to track my cycling activities, and an app called Fitbod to help me accomplish my weight training goals. Using these apps helped me make myself accountable and transform my body into something to be proud of. These are just a few resources to help you get started and stay active.

But the first step is the most important—and only you can take that step.

24

Numbers Don't Lie

Even When People Do

As a survivor, I don't have the luxury of being lax with my diet because I have already found out the hard way the dangers of bad eating habits, and I may not be as lucky again. What's more, I can't hide this from my doctors.

Since the heart attack, I have had at least a yearly visit to the lipid clinic. If my numbers are more concerning than expected, that triggers an extra visit for the year. I made all my appointments after the heart attack to be sure I was staying on top of my health and catching any more issues early so that we could address them quickly. During these visits, I have my blood tested, looking not just at cholesterol but also at my blood pressure, sugar levels, and kidney and liver function to ensure everything works properly. I have the chance to discuss treatment with my medical team and make a plan for anything new we should try or cut from my treatment plan.

At first, I visited the clinic twice yearly for a checkup, usually every six months. But one particular visit served as my wake-up call after I had begun slacking on my treatment. This visit was scheduled for the fall, which was already bad for me, mainly because it was right after my wedding and honeymoon.

I forgot about a diet or restrictions because I was too busy enjoying the moments and memories. I knew that—and could explain it—but no matter what I said or how I tried to downplay things, I could never escape the results.

As they say,

"Men lie, women lie, but numbers don't lie."

No matter how I tried to spin things, I couldn't fake my lab results. I might have omitted how many hot dogs and burgers I had at the BBQ, or skipped sharing that I indulged too much in Southern cooking, eating more than one plate of all types of foods that would impact my numbers. But no matter what I said, the numbers would always tell the truth.

During my appointments, I built rapport and trust with one nurse practitioner. In a large and busy hospital chain like the Cleveland Clinic, which is the second-best hospital in the world by reputation, it can sometimes be a bit harder to navigate your care. I have a medical doctor who is my doctor on paper, but I have seen his nurse practitioner much more over the years. The idea of a nurse practitioner as a leading medical professional made me skeptical because, like many people, I considered the doctor the primary source of medical information.

At first, it took a while, but eventually, I developed trust with her, dropping my guard and allowing her in—not just my numbers, but also my lifestyle—so we could create the best health care plan for me. Admittedly, being honest during our first visits was hard because I still lied to myself—again, like an addict who refuses to believe they have a problem. Deep down, I knew I could be better, but I wasn't ready to be better, and my numbers reflected that, leading my NP to repeat a suggestion she had been making for the past couple of visits:

"I think it's time to start you on Repatha."

She had been mentioning this drug for quite a while, but this time, with my results, I thought it was best to listen and consider it. The NP went on to explain what it was and how it worked. Repatha is a PCSK9 inhibitor, a medication that lowers LDL cholesterol in the blood. It works by blocking a protein called PCSK9 (proprotein convertase subtilisin/kexin type 9), which helps the liver remove LDL cholesterol from the blood.

Repatha comes as an injectable, so I would have to inject myself twice a month. At the time, there was little information on side effects, which was my largest red flag and hesitation. I struggled with the thought of being on this medication for life. I constantly weighed whether it was worth holding out or going for it, as managing my cholesterol had proven more difficult than I thought. I feared potential side effects that might be discovered after years of use.

But my numbers weren't ideal for a survivor, putting me at risk for another event. My overall cholesterol was 242 (over the standard 200 threshold), and my LDL was 172—for heart attack patients, guidelines target under 70.

I wasn't surprised. I knew I was not only falling off the wagon but slow to get back on it. I had let myself slide, secretly hoping that the two separate cholesterol medications I was taking would do the heavy lifting for me. I was becoming too lax with my diet, thinking a pill could cover for my bad habits. But the numbers cut straight through my excuses and told the real story. Even with the medication, my cholesterol was still too high.

The last thing I wanted was another medication, especially when it felt optional. I questioned whether the NP's office received incentives for prescribing it—especially since Repatha had only been on the market a couple of years, with limited long-term data beyond clinical trials. I felt like one of the youngest people starting this medication—after a heart attack, and when the drug was brand new—and worried I'd be the canary in the coal mine for side effects.

Still, the NP claimed, "In the patients who have been on it, it has worked wonders." I wasn't ready to go down that road yet, but this was the moment I realized I couldn't fake the numbers, and to do better, I had to be better. I made a deal with the NP and told her I would adopt as many lifestyle changes as I could realistically maintain.

I started to get caught up in my youth, fearing that I would miss out on delicious foods and enjoyable meals, but I had to let go of thoughts like, *Is it too early to be this strict about my diet?* This is where the concept of controlling the controllables helped me focus more than ever. I wanted to prove to the doctor and myself that I could lower my cholesterol without new medicines—I was already on five, from cholesterol and blood pressure meds to preventive medicines to lower my chances of another heart attack. I certainly didn't want to add a sixth.

The goal was to reduce my medicines, not add more. I had six months to accomplish this with changes I could live with forever. I didn't plan to go entirely vegan, but I got serious about moderation and making sure my overall diet was heart-healthy. Worst case, if I didn't reach my goal, I would concede, put my fears aside, and fully accept Repatha.

I had to face my addiction head-on. The first thing I had to do was be honest with myself. I had to admit that I had a problem and an unhealthy relationship with food. In facing that fact, I was able to implement a strict lifestyle change—not to be confused with a diet. A lifestyle change is much different; it's permanent, while diets are usually temporary.

Knowing the difference can save you from disappointment and failure. A diet typically focuses on a specific aspect, such as what you eat. It's often a plan with rules about what foods to include and exclude and in what quantities. Diets are usually time-limited, lasting anywhere from a few days to several months.

Diets include keto, Paleo, Atkins, intermittent fasting (which can be a lifestyle change for some but is often approached as temporary), and other specific weight-loss programs. Diets often revolve around a big event, and after the end date, most people revert to their old habits, often erasing the progress they made.

On the other hand, a lifestyle change focuses on creating healthy habits that become natural parts of daily life. This leads to more gradual but more sustainable and profound improvements in health and well-being over the long term. For instance, I didn't completely cut out French fries, my favorite. But I limited myself to one fried food per month—fries or anything else fried. That way, I could still enjoy my favorites but stay mindful of fried intake overall.

Returning to *moderation*, which means balance and restraint: Salads suddenly became more frequent, and fast food became virtually nonexistent. I finally started to get ahead of my fast-food addiction. I began focusing on cooking again and making better food choices.

The more I resisted fast food, the easier it became.

It was a sacrifice, but necessary to prove I could control the controllables enough to avoid extra medicines. I was working out, eating right, and taking my medications on time. I was patient with myself. I stopped beating myself up over bad choices and committed to doing better next time. I reminded myself that this is a marathon, not a sprint. Most importantly, I was honest about my triggers and stayed away, tuning into myself, being serious about self-discipline, and taking back the control that my fast-food addiction had had over me.

February came along, and I was ready to prove my NP wrong. I had even dropped a few pounds I didn't know I could lose. I was locked in, and I became even more confident that this was a lifestyle change I could maintain for the rest of my life. I had been doing everything right and was eager for my test results to reflect that, proving once and for all that these medicines weren't necessary.

As expected, my cholesterol levels decreased by forty-three points overall. That got me below the high threshold of two hundred. My LDL dropped by twenty-nine points, which might seem like a cause for celebration, but my numbers were still off. Forty-three points took my cholesterol from 242 to 199, only one point away from 200. My LDL went from 172 to 143, still extremely high for a survivor and a concern for my medical team.

I had done everything possible, controlled what I could, adhered to a strict diet, and remained consistent with my workouts. But the fact is, even when you do all you can, you can't beat genetics. I was only thirty-two then and still considered myself to have a lot of life ahead of me. But I am also a man of my word.

I didn't want to get on this medication, but I couldn't live the life I wanted without its help. The only thing that could have helped was going plant-based, but that wasn't even a guarantee I would see the results I wanted. So I accepted.

The results from one test to the next were indeed night and day. After six months of seeing how my body would react to my lifestyle changes plus Repatha, my numbers went from 199 to 110 overall, and my LDL from 142 to 33—proving that, to beat an addiction, you have to be honest with yourself and accept help.

The Doctor Dilemma

Navigating and Healing from Negative Encounters

At thirty-five years old—seven years after my heart attack and four years into taking Repatha, the so-called miracle cholesterol drug, and sticking to a consistent workout routine—I was still told, "You could die" by a medical professional during a routine checkup. Hearing those words stunned me. Normally, I would have spiraled into self-blame, picked apart everything I might have done wrong, or let myself feel defeated. But this time, I didn't. For the first time, I felt good about my treatment plan.

That confidence led me to a realization I think many people can relate to: Sometimes, what we hear in the doctor's office isn't the whole picture. Even well-meaning doctors can get it wrong, or their words can land more harshly than intended. This was the first time since my heart attack when I truly believed the doctor's warning didn't add up. I was confused—despite working this hard and keeping up with medications, I was still hearing I could die. What else could I possibly do?

On December 7, 2022, I was scheduled for a routine visit to the lipid clinic. By this time, my progress had changed, and I was in tune with my body. I was so in sync that I could quickly recognize and identify when something was off. I knew when I was indulging in certain things too much or if I was lacking in a specific area. I was confident going into this appointment, thinking it was a formality. Plus, this time, I had the Repatha on my side.

The NP I usually saw wasn't available, so she referred me to someone else in the office. The office has a medical team specializing in preventive cardiology, including cholesterol management. Since it was all within the same office and I trusted my NP completely, I quickly followed her suggestion without hesitation. That's because, for once, I had allowed myself to trust my medical team entirely, and the NP I had been seeing was a big reason for this. She was the first medical professional who walked me through my treatment, clearly explaining things to me, presenting the pros and cons to consider, and offering her best medical opinion. Most of all, she allowed me to make a no-pressure decision and supported me regardless of what I decided.

As I mentioned earlier, during our appointments, my NP and I had started to develop a friendly relationship. We would briefly talk about things ranging from work to family. I would ask about her children; she was pregnant a few times during my visits. She gave birth to at least two children during the years I saw her. Likewise, she took an interest in my life, asking about milestones like my engagement and wedding. These conversations allowed me to open up and feel more comfortable around her. We even reached a point where a couple of my jokes would land and make her laugh.

Through small talk, light jokes, and building comfort, I became more honest about my body. I started to worry less about judgment or expecting bad news when I had overindulged, and instead, I focused on solutions rather than hiding my problems. That included being honest about the amount of wine I drink in a week—because little things like that matter. Without open and honest dialogue, getting proper treatment and getting on the right track are more challenging.

Opening up helped me receive better advice that improved my test results and overall health. This experience taught me the importance of open and honest communication in health care, empowering me to share my concerns and enabling my health care team to provide the best care possible. I committed to staying on top of my treatment and consistently seeing the same professionals, who had a complete profile on me to ensure I still received the best care, regardless of who among them I saw.

My visits with my NP had become so pleasant that they completely changed my viewpoint about health and wellness. I started to seek out other medical treatments and opinions, and address other lingering medical issues. I gathered the courage to reach out and find a primary care doctor. Before, I thought doctors were all the same. I thought I'd be okay if I just stayed up with my cardiology and cholesterol appointments. However, I was overlooking the fact that different doctors specialize in different areas; consulting a doctor within their field is the best way to receive the most effective treatment. For me, a primary care doctor is the one who can identify an issue and recommend a specialist if needed.

I started getting everything checked out, from major health issues to minor problems and small annoyances that corrective surgery could fix. I fully trust my medical team's decisions and believe they provide the best care. This experience taught me the importance of seeking specialized treatments, empowering me to explore my health care options and ensure I receive the best possible care. While most of my experiences have been positive, I also learned that one variable can never be predicted: people.

This brings us back to my visit to the lipid clinic. After I checked in, I sat and waited for my name to be called. I didn't know who to look out for, as this was an appointment with someone new. Shortly after my name was called, as I went to greet the new nurse practitioner, I noticed the energy was off. It felt as if she were giving off tension and nervous energy, as if I were someone she wasn't expecting. Her welcome immediately made me feel uncomfortable. She seemed to be in a rush, and her tone was abrupt. Since I had gone to the same NP for years, I may have forgotten the awkward feeling of meeting a medical professional for the first time.

It almost felt like starting over, much like getting back into the dating scene after ending a long-term relationship. It was just one visit, but the number of questions I had to answer and the backstory I had to share was exhausting. It made me appreciate going to a medical professional who knows me. The same nervous energy with which I was greeted persisted throughout the visit, causing the NP's answers to be quick and without much thought. The surprise of learning that I had suffered a heart attack at such a young age didn't help, as she reacted with actual shock and gave me advice as if the heart attack had happened a short time before the visit. Even as she reviewed my numbers and asked questions, she eventually said,

"If you don't work out daily, you will die."

Upon hearing that, my first thought was to shut down—to just nod and smile at whatever she said next, to speed up my visit. But no, I decided in that moment not to let this shake my confidence. I had finally gotten my cholesterol numbers to a manageable level. I was highly active, biking, running, and working out regularly. And most of all, I was improving my diet—ish. There's always room for improvement, but it wasn't bad enough to warrant those words.

"But that's only if you have numbers showing you could have diabetes," she clarified after sensing my reaction through my nonverbal cues. That made her take another look at my chart, only to realize she had misread it.

When she took my blood pressure, it was higher than usual. That could have easily resulted from the anxiety and discomfort I felt at the moment, and I tried to explain that to her; she still reacted based on my results and not my words. Her solution was to increase the dosage of one of my medications. Even though I told her it wasn't necessary, eventually, she prescribed it anyway and mentioned that we would discuss the results at my six-month follow-up. But there was no need for that because I exercised my right as a patient to request never to see her again.

While it might seem harsh, mental health is just as vital as physical health. Telling patients they could die if they miss a workout is extremely irresponsible. Such scare tactics might discourage people from seeking medical attention, which ultimately harms the individual, not the doctor. Especially with sensitive topics like health, a careful approach is essential.

Building a strong and trusting relationship with your medical team is an investment in your long-term health and well-being. It allows for better communication, personalized care, improved outcomes, and a greater sense of support. Now, more than ever, websites, mobile apps, and screening clinics allow people to shop for medical professionals and get a second opinion. Even if you select a doctor and it doesn't work out, you don't have to stay. It's essential to shop around for the right provider you trust, who has good reviews in their specialty.

You know you've found the right doctor when:

- They are knowledgeable and provide thorough assessments.

- They can clearly explain your issues in a way that doesn't intimidate you.

- They present the latest treatment options and are informed about current trends, studies, and advancements.

- They tailor your treatment to you, instead of using a one-size-fits-all approach.

And, most importantly, a good doctor can acknowledge and help you process your emotions as you make medical decisions. They understand that tough choices regarding your health sometimes have to be made, and they do so with empathy and patience. They are with you every step of the way, supporting your choices and reminding you that you're in this together.

These are the things I had to remember from my bad experience with this nurse practitioner. The visit felt nostalgic but in a negative way. It brought back memories of times when I didn't trust doctors because I thought they exaggerated everything. Fearmongering and blindly prescribing unnecessary medication just because that's the standard recommendation—rather than taking the time to understand the patient and make the best suggestion for them—has left a bad taste in many people's mouths. Even simple things, like long wait times, lectures about health facts you already know, or more serious issues like a dreaded medical diagnosis or a poor bedside manner, are among the usual complaints from people who haven't been to the doctor in years, aside from the fear of medical costs.

But we must all remember that doctors are here to help, not harm. Medical professionals are reminded of this when they take the Hippocratic oath—a foundational ethical pledge affirming their commitment to patient care, professional conduct, and the moral responsibilities of medicine. Nurses take the Nightingale pledge, a modified version of the Hippocratic oath tailored specifically for nurses.

While these professionals take these pledges and the expectation is that they care wholeheartedly, one fact remains: The variable is always people. We may not always have the best experiences, but remember, you can always find another health care professional. You are the customer, and your medical staff is working for you. You might not find the right team on the first try, but keep searching until you find the best team—one committed to keeping you around as long as possible.

26

From the Deep Fryer to the Air Fryer

Deciding what to eat became a daily mental tug-of-war the moment I got serious about my lifestyle change. Knowing what I now knew about the food I had eaten for most of my life was like finding out Santa Claus wasn't real—except this time, discovering the truth could actually hurt me. It was disappointing—painful, even—to realize that a lot of the foods I grew up loving were filled with ingredients that could literally kill me if I wasn't careful.

Reading food labels became a daily ritual that left me frustrated and overwhelmed. It felt like everything I touched had a hidden danger lurking beneath. Suddenly, just walking through the grocery store turned into a chemistry test I hadn't studied for. There were days I thought, *Is there anything left I can safely eat?* That's when I came across something different—something that would change the way I approached food entirely: the air fryer.

It started casually, just scrolling on Instagram when I came across a post from a friend, showing off their new air fryer and a picture of foods I'd told myself I could no longer eat. Things like wings, fries, and even crispy chicken—all made without deep-frying. As I was struggling to find healthy alternatives for comfort foods, I was intrigued. Honestly, I had nothing to lose because, at that point, everything I loved had landed on the "Don't eat it" list. But before I bought one, I wanted to know exactly what it was.

It turns out that air fryers are small countertop appliances that cook food by rapidly circulating hot air around it, giving the food a crisp outer layer while requiring little to no oil. It fries, bakes, and roasts. When I explain it to my friends, I always say it's like an Easy-Bake Oven for grown-ups.

Before I could hit "Buy now," my mom beat me to it. Always listening, always helping without hovering—she surprised me with an air fryer for Christmas. At first, it was just a creative way to reintroduce some of my favorite meals—especially French fries, which had been one of my strongest weaknesses.

French fries, as comforting as they are, have become one of the biggest red flags in my journey to a heart-healthy lifestyle. I used to think fries were simple—just potatoes in oil, maybe some salt. But I found out that fries from some major fast-food chains contain up to nineteen ingredients. Nineteen. For fries. That's when I knew something wasn't right. Most of these added ingredients are focused on consistency, shelf life, and branding—which means their priority is flavor and appearance, not your health.

What should be just potatoes, oil, and salt suddenly has a whole chemistry book attached. Beef flavoring is often added, which makes them not actually vegetarian. There is dextrose, a sugar that gives fries their golden color and helps with preservation. Citric acid helps maintain the fryer oil, while sodium acid pyrophosphate keeps the fries from turning gray in storage.

And then the names got scarier—tertiary butylhydroquinone (TBHQ) and dimethylpolysiloxane, the kinds of compounds that sound like they belong in a science lab instead of my takeout bag. One is used to prevent oxidation in oil; the other prevents foaming. Funny thing is, if you saw "TBHQ" on a science quiz, you'd guess it's a new planet—or a chemical weapon.

But it isn't just fries. I started digging through ingredient lists for things like frozen pizzas, cheeseburgers, Chinese takeout, and even canned soups. These hidden chemical names began to appear everywhere: phthalates, MSG, potassium sorbate, and sodium benzoate. Even though the FDA labels some of these as "generally recognized as safe," that doesn't mean they are truly safe for me—especially as someone trying to keep my heart alive and working.

In cardiac recovery, they taught us a simple rule: If there are more than five ingredients you can't pronounce, it's probably not something your body wants. And I started seeing not just five but ten, fifteen, sometimes more in the foods that were once everyday items. The anxiety this triggered pushed me to get serious about cooking and understanding everything I was putting into my body. That's another way I learned to control the controllables.

The air fryer helped shift everything. It allowed me to catch up on meals I missed but with healthier ingredients—foods that are lower in oil, reduced in fat, and still full of flavor. It gave me back the texture I craved from fried food without the guilt. I started simply: potatoes, a light coat of olive oil, and a sprinkle of kosher salt. Just three ingredients. No hidden chemicals. No headaches or regrets afterward.

Of course, the early experiments weren't perfect. In fact, they were often a mess. Food would come out undercooked or not crispy enough. Cooking times were inconsistent, and I even forgot to shake the basket once or twice—only to discover that the top half was done, while the rest looked raw. I had to research temperatures, learn the timing, and figure things out through trial and error. This was also before air fryers were as mainstream as they are now, so my support system was basically YouTube and stubborn determination.

But I stuck with it. I wasn't going back. And eventually, something transformed: not just the food but my approach as well. I became what I now proudly call a "five-star air fryer chef.

Today, I don't crave fast food as much as I used to. I've recreated healthier versions of all my favorites: ribs, wings, chicken, even fried catfish—every dish tied to a memory, a moment, or a person. Some meals were nods to "sauce on everything" versions of my past. My air-fried ribs fall off the bone and taste like something from back in the day—without the layers of regret. My air-fried chicken? Golden and crispy, made with breadcrumbs and olive oil instead of heavy oil and flour. It's about 50 percent fewer calories but still tastes like something you'd buy at a soul food spot on a Sunday afternoon.

Even my catfish recipe—one I associate with my Uncle Mike and our family gatherings—got an air fryer version that I can eat with pride. It's still full of flavor but now made in a way that aligns with my goals.

Today, we have two air fryers at home—because one just wasn't enough. With most of our meals needing multiple parts or portions, upgrading was an easy decision. I'll never forget the sight of hot, fresh chicken breasts cooking in one air fryer while the second works on baked potatoes. The digital timer buzzes just in time to remind us when to flip or check our food, giving us space to focus on preparing vegetables to complete the meal. Everything comes out perfectly cooked—at just the right temperature—and with the two air fryers running, the cooking time is cut in half. Recreating our favorites in the air fryer quietly reduced our fast-food cravings before we even realized it. Air fryers aren't just niche gadgets anymore; they're now being built into ovens and ranges, becoming part of the mainstream conversation around convenience and healthy eating.

I've become something of an accidental spokesperson. I don't sell them, but the DMs and conversations I've had with people trying to turn their lives around, or just eat a little better, are worth more than any brand endorsement. If I can inspire someone to take one small step—learning a new recipe, ditching a fast-food habit, or simply dusting off the appliance they received for Christmas—then I consider that a win. Every time I pick up the air fryer basket, I'm reminded that small changes can fuel a major comeback. That's exactly what the air fryer has given me—a way to enjoy so many foods I love, while still taking care of my health.

Granted, overeating is still its own challenge. But I've started being intentional about saving food for tomorrow, learning to savor instead of overindulge. Sharing my air fryer creations on social media has become its own source of accountability—the likes, the feedback, and the challenge to get more creative each time keep me motivated to move forward.

This tool, this habit, this mindset—they're all just another way to live heart-first and stay #HeartStrong.

"Babe, Do You Really Need Another Plate?"

Accountability Is a Love Language

Well, this is embarrassing, but in the spirit of transparency, I should admit this: In 2023, I still indulged in some foods more than I should have. I still caught myself from time to time eating some of those dangerously good-tasting foods that aren't the best for me, but it was more than that. I started to develop an issue with portion control.

Usually, we cook to have leftovers for the next day. Sometimes I would forget that and go back for seconds, thirds, or even fourths. I was losing sight of the fact that, even though I was cooking at home and it was healthier, I was still overeating. While I was making progress, I was making twice as many excuses. With the medication I was on and working out, I underestimated what moderation looked like. I was losing focus, and Alexis noticed.

Although my takeout food consumption was much lower than ever before, overeating still contributed to weight gain alongside my overindulgence in homemade meals. Picture eating a family-sized pack of chicken, a box of store-bought rice, and vegetables. Overeating can have negative consequences even when your diet consists mainly of healthy foods. The healthiness of a food does not always eliminate the effects of overeating it. Regular overeating disrupts the hormones that regulate hunger and fullness, leading to persistent weight gain and increasing the risk of obesity issues. Plus, it's just too much food.

In the past, Alexis has confronted me directly when I've slipped on my food choices or eaten way more than I needed. Still, I would fire back with excuses, leading to uncomfortable confrontations and triggering insecure feelings within myself. My responses were from a place of guilt, knowing I shouldn't be eating certain things or overeating something. I was unable to handle facing my failures so bluntly. But Alexis didn't give up; she just changed her approach. Instead of a callout, she challenged me.

It was the start of 2023, and Alexis caught me slipping. I was digging into a fried catfish meal with fries and hushpuppies—something I thought I had every once in a blue moon, but Alexis noticed it was more than usual. We had established our cooking regimen and a plan to prepare healthy meals at home. Still, several times, we both convinced ourselves that we were too tired to cook, or it was too late. By now, Alexis knew me well enough to know I wouldn't have taken being called out lightly, but to her credit, that didn't stop her from finding a way to voice her concern.

"You know, you should see if you can stop eating fried foods until your next doctor's appointment."

My upcoming appointment was supposed to be a significant one for me. My numbers had started to rise again. Whenever that happened, I doubled down on my lifestyle and kept a close eye on things. She could see in real time what was happening, so she used the moment to motivate me. Secretly, this was a brilliant approach. With that statement, Alexis took away my ability to be offended and lash out in guilt. Instead, she made it a challenge, making me see things differently.

"Okay, bet. I can do that," I replied.

Was it going to be difficult? Absolutely, but it was a challenge worth taking on. I wanted to prove to Alexis and myself that it could be done. Overcoming something like this would be an achievement. It all motivated me to keep working toward better health.

Alexis is my accountability partner for things like this. Accountability partners support you in reaching your goals by holding you responsible for your actions. They check in, offer encouragement, and help keep you on track. Knowing someone else knows your goals and expects updates creates good external pressure. You're not just accountable to yourself, which makes it harder to ignore tasks or give up when things get tough. Research shows that simply telling someone about your goals increases your chances of achieving them. Alexis has always found a way, no matter how tough the callout. One of her favorite subtle warnings is when she notices I am starting to mindlessly go back for multiple rounds of food.

"Babe, do you really need another plate?"

Whenever I hear that, I understand what she is trying to communicate, even through her indirect way of telling me I've gained some weight. Another way she manages to alert me that I am slipping is by saying something like, "You're starting to look tubby." She tends to be more direct when she is annoyed with me. But no matter how she says it, the message serves as motivation. It's a call for me to start focusing, lock in, and return to being healthy.

Accountability in the household has become a two-way street. Although I may struggle with food, I have remained consistent with my workout routine. My consistency in working out has motivated Alexis to join me. I usually get up four days a week around 6:30 a.m. to go to the gym. Alexis isn't a morning person, but when she feels me leave the bed and hears me say, "It's time," she separates from the comfortable bed and warm pillows to get ready. She has admitted that she probably wouldn't get up that early if it weren't for my going to the gym. Knowing she depends on me motivates me to stay consistent and ensure we both make it to the gym.

But you don't have to limit yourself to just one accountability partner. The first example of accountability partners I remember is my involvement with Run with the Winners. The group's competitive spirit and genuine connection kept us honest in our running efforts. Although it can be a competitive group, it remains low-pressure. This sense of community and support has been invaluable in my journey toward better health. I encourage you to find that too.

I have even made my social media followers my accountability partners, especially when it comes to encouraging them to work out. I include interactive polls in my Instagram stories for my followers to answer, such as "Did you go to the gym today?" I use social media to connect with people nearby and to remind them to take time for themselves and exercise. Using hashtags and creating fun, engaging challenges is a great way to get people involved.

I've been invited to challenges. Those are always fun because these movements are enjoyable and can save lives. Usually, to join these challenges, you must complete a task, such as working out, and post a picture on your personal account as proof, tagging the person who challenged you. Not only does this serve as your digital receipt, but it also encourages others to join the challenge.

Using #HeartStrong is an excellent example of this. When my followers see it, it reminds them of my heart attack and the importance of making small decisions to care for themselves. You should live and love life to the fullest, but make small choices to help ensure a long life. I've often been told that my posts and story have inspired many people. People have reported that after seeing my message, they started working out, became more proactive about doctor visits, and made lifestyle changes. Sharing my personal story has empowered others to take control of their health and make positive changes in their lives. Not to mention, challenges and hashtags also play into the herd mentality—but in a positive way. Herd mentality is a psychological phenomenon in which individuals in a group adopt the behaviors, beliefs, or attitudes of the majority, sometimes even overriding their own personal judgment or individuality. Sometimes people see this as a bad thing, but the #HeartStrong movement is an example that it's not always bad.

In this case, seeing others participate in challenges makes it seem cool and popular. That, mixed with FOMO—fear of missing out—can quickly get people involved when they don't want to feel left out. Just like with Run with the Winners, viral health challenges can promote inclusivity, create a support group, and make people feel like part of a larger group or community. And most of all, everybody is at least a little competitive, so most people answer when tagged or challenged. However, it's all in good spirit and fun—and it ultimately leads back to people being active and moving.

After my experience, I developed an even deeper, genuine care for others. Sharing my story has allowed others to open up about their health. In listening to their stories, I help people recognize what may have happened to them to avoid more serious issues down the line. My favorite part is hearing the success stories: catching a problem early, getting treatment, or following through on weight-loss journeys inspired by the #HeartStrong movement. Using the hashtag is a way to keep people accountable and dedicated to a cause. It brings joy to my heart and reminds people to focus more on what's in *their* hearts.

I also check in mentally with the people who share their health journeys with me, becoming someone who can hold them accountable and encourage them to stay on track. Even for those who haven't shared their personal stories, I remind people as often as possible that when you're ready, you don't have to do this alone. The callouts and challenges I promote aren't just for working out but also include cooking, mental health, and well-being—anything that involves taking time for yourself. Challenges provide people with motivation, purpose, and a sense of accomplishment when they achieve their goals.

Which brings me back to my bet with Alexis. I took her offer and put aside deep-fried foods completely. Surprisingly, it was easier than I thought, maybe because I had already been phasing out these foods. Alexis and I never formally discussed what this bet looked like, what the stakes were, or what the wagers were. But we didn't need to, because the real stake was my life.

To win my bet with myself, I quit French fries completely for six months. That meant avoiding places where fries were the default side—even if I wasn't ordering a burger, the temptation was too strong. I chose restaurants with better options, like salads or veggies, instead. I've since gone back to fast food occasionally and broken my one-fried-food-per-month rule more times than I'd like to admit. But now I cook homemade air fryer fries or 40% reduced-fat chips at home—still fries, but smarter choices that satisfy without the full guilt.

Without fried foods, my calorie intake dropped immediately, and I saw positive results in my body. A small patch of fat began to melt away. The excuse had been that it was there due to age. The fact was that it was there because of poor food choices. During this period, I really got back into cooking at home. Those moments when I thought it was so easy to just get fast food instead of cooking at home have changed. Instead of pulling up to the drive-through at 9 p.m., I find myself rushing to the grocery store before it closes to get the last item I need to complete my meal. I am getting creative with more dishes. I've perfected all the "fried foods" in my air fryer—from air-fried chicken with the perfect flavor and crunch to fries that would give any local restaurant a run for its money. Most importantly, we perfected the perfect fry right at home. Everything is so fresh and flavorful that my urge to eat out has dropped significantly.

All this was confirmed when I got my test results back from my NP. My numbers were back on track, exactly where we hoped. Not only did I complete the challenge, but I also made it a lifestyle change. Now, I have way fewer fried foods than ever before. I'm serious about it. The only times I indulge are when I genuinely deserve it and am practicing moderation or when I'm on vacation, enjoying a moment with my wife. My rule is simple: Is this an experience or just a habit? I'll enjoy a unique local dish while traveling or a celebration meal with family, but I no longer grab greasy fast food just because it's convenient or I'm stressed. That is where I draw the line.

Alexis presented me with a challenge, and in return, I help others to be their best—just as she does for me. Accountability isn't a one-person job; sometimes it takes a village. Accountability partners can be family, coworkers, sponsors, teammates—anybody who cares enough to invest in your goals with you. Even if they find creative ways to call you out without hurting your feelings, their support can be everything.

Healing Those Hopeless Prayers
Because Faith Without Works...Can Kill You

Some say *love* is the most overused, misused, and even abused word in the English language. But I'd argue that *hope* is a close second. We lean too heavily on hope—it's everywhere: in our conversations, in our advertisements, in our slogans. It's a word we hold close, using it as both a verb and an attitude. For many, including myself, hope becomes a saving grace. I've been guilty of that. Even when I saw the warning signs about my health—clear, loud, and undeniable—I still clung to hope, believing somehow things would turn out differently for me. I didn't know what would save me—medicine, fate, pure luck—but I thought hope would. I used it not to spark action but to avoid reality. And the harsh truth is, while hope can inspire, when misused—just like love—it can hurt you. It can even kill you. Facing health issues head-on isn't just important; it's essential. It's the first step in breaking the generational curses we've ignored for too long—curses that hide in plain sight, masked by the excuses we've normalized.

Hope can heal, or hope can hurt.

Putting off my health concerns until I was "older" wasn't difficult at all. It seemed normal. My father had heart disease. So did my sister. So when it was my turn, I felt strangely comforted, even justified. It was almost like a rite of passage—something we all carried. No one in my family ever really pressed me about my cholesterol numbers. We all assumed this was just how life was for us—that medication would eventually be the answer, and we'd handle things when the time came. So when I finally started paying attention to my health, I hoped the newest drugs and my workout routine would be enough.

I convinced myself I still had time to live freely, on my own terms. That with just a little effort, I could outrun the inevitable. But the truth? I was in denial. Deep down, I believed I might somehow be the exception, that all this might just skip me. Obviously, it didn't, but the feeling of hope I had made me a believer because I was taught that my God can overcome anything—my mother would often tell me that, just like others in the family. And sometimes, having faith was just enough to keep us going, with no worries.

Even the thought of visiting the doctor irritated me. Since I didn't have a primary care doctor during my college years, each visit to the doctor felt like *Fifty First Dates*. Answering the same questions repeatedly forced me to talk about my father and his death. With every interaction, there was always a reaction. Most would react upon hearing about my father's multiple heart attacks, a stroke, and his death at an early age. With each reaction, I grew more numb to their responses. While I should have taken these reactions more seriously, I started to ignore and dismiss them as scare tactics to make me eat better. Plus, I had what I thought was faith but was really just blind optimism, a passive hope that everything would work out without me having to do the work.

Faith is often described as complete trust or confidence in someone or something. While the word usually evokes thoughts of religion, faith extends beyond spirituality—it can also be grounded in our experiences, the testimony of others, and a profound inner conviction. Rather than being blind or unfounded, faith often draws strength from what we've seen in the past and what we know now. It is this willingness to trust—sometimes without absolute certainty—that shapes both our beliefs and our actions.

Faith can be used to shield ourselves from hard feelings—fear, anxiety, even guilt.

Faith, in terms of religion, has always been a significant part of our family, going back to the days when my grandfather wouldn't let us miss church in Northport, and my father made sure God was at the center of everything we did. So even when we weren't attending church regularly, our faith stayed strong. This was especially true during the deaths of my father and sister.

Our faith had played a key role in shaping our expectations about my father's and my sister's health and healing. The doctors had given my father two weeks to live, but that didn't make sense because we believed he would beat the odds. My sister Jocelyn's father-in-law, who is a doctor himself, had told the family that Jocelyn would most likely pass away, delivering the devastating news before her actual doctor even brought up the conversation. Despite his being a highly experienced, world-renowned doctor, my family still rejected his claim because, according to my mother, "We are a praying family, and he does not truly know the power of *our* God."

Even recalling my doctor's visit at twenty-six years old, I stopped taking my newly prescribed cholesterol medications because I *hoped* that taking them for a short time would buy me more time to avoid the doctor, or even worse, avoid the same fate as my father. I felt like all I could do was wait and see how long I could avoid confronting my problems and how far my faith would carry me. This distinction is crucial. Confusing hope and faith is common for many people when it comes to their health care. As ethicists Steve Clarke and colleagues note, patients' conviction-based hopes (religious or otherwise) can lead them to unrealistic expectations of treatment success, causing delays or refusal of recommended care in favor of unattainable outcomes or miracles.

While I do believe in miracles, and they do happen, they are not a medical treatment.

I used my faith to hide my fear, which paralyzed me from taking real action. I was hoping for a miracle regarding my future health outcomes. Not realizing at the time that I was confusing my faith with hope, I thought hope was a feeling of expectation and desire for something to happen. The focus here is on the sense of anticipation and the possibility of something happening in the future. While hope is driven by desire, past experiences, and trust, even in the absence of conviction, faith is driven by a deep inner knowing and the courage to act on it.

There is a term for this. The Saint Luke Institute refers to it as spiritualizing. This happens when people use their faith or spirituality to avoid dealing with challenging personal issues, like fear, anxiety, or insecurity. Instead of facing these complex feelings directly, they might rely on faith-based explanations or activities to suppress or hide the underlying fear. This process can be unconscious, meaning individuals may truly believe they are expressing faith when, in reality, they're using it to shield themselves from painful emotions. However, recognizing and addressing this can help lead to better outcomes and more informed decision-making.

Even when people are aware of historical family issues, some still tend to rely on miracles, which only continues the cycle of ignorance. Sometimes ignorance is easier than facing the truth. To be clear, I am not saying that having faith when dealing with serious medical conditions is ignorant, but

having faith without works could kill you.

Speaking of family, James 2:17 warns, "Faith by itself, if it is not accompanied by action, is dead"—a subtle shoutout to the faith my family instilled in me when I was young.

But what are works? In this case, works are the actions you need to take to seek treatment. For some, like me, it also includes trusting God alongside those actions, such as praying for peace while awaiting a diagnosis. You did the work by seeing the doctor; prayer brings comfort, knowing God helps you conquer. At first, I only prayed without follow-through, creating false hope and misplaced faith.

Misplaced faith means trusting prayer over medical action, perpetuating the cycle of hoping instead of helping. When bad news hits, and you feel powerless, faith becomes the last resort. For me, with a broken body and no fixes, I dropped to my knees, praying for mercy.

Having misplaced or false faith also makes it easier to ignore serious warnings and signs that could save your life if treated early. Eventually, that false faith or hope causes people to normalize problematic situations, leading to a phenomenon known as normalcy bias. Normalcy bias is a cognitive bias that causes people to doubt or downplay threat warnings. As a result, individuals often underestimate the likelihood of experiencing a disaster and its potential harm. Understanding the severity of health issues is not just important; it's essential, as this knowledge empowers you to take the right steps to manage and treat them effectively.

When these potential dangers come up in conversation, the person experiencing bias usually responds calmly, saying things as I did: "Is that really going to happen?" or "It won't be that bad." These statements are ways to convince themselves and others that things will always go as planned. Even if presented with evidence, the person experiencing bias still finds a way to work around it. We avoid our problems because we don't see the test results from the doctor, but the issues still exist if you continue to play hide-and-seek with your health.

When I arrived at the hospital on the day of my heart attack, the EMS workers and ER doctors both told me, "We think you had a heart attack." But I had a hard time accepting the news, responding as if I had been arguing, as if I had been tagged in a game of hide-and-seek, dismissing the seriousness of the situation. "Yeah, right. I am way too young for that." I was absolutely sure the doctors were wrong because I felt great, and since I thought a heart attack was supposed to be "worse," I was sure it was a misdiagnosis. I wasn't ready to quit my game or admit defeat, even if it could cost me my life.

If you're dealing with a genetic issue, you're not alone. The CDC estimates 1 in 33 babies (3%) are born with birth defects, many genetic. Genetic conditions affect millions worldwide. From high blood pressure to cancer, most Americans, especially Black Americans, live with these diseases and know they tend to run in families. While I disliked talking to doctors about my health problems, I found comfort in hearing from others who suffered similar conditions. Through our conversations, my issues felt more common and easier to accept as part of life, much like generations before me did, until the problems became too much to ignore.

Later in life, through reflection, I realized that normalizing our health issues is a form of a generational curse. Usually, these curses are hard to recognize because people grow up around these behaviors or environments and begin to adopt them over time. The small things you unconsciously pick up from your parents could lead to health risks later on. While some common curses are alcoholism, abuse, and adultery, maybe the biggest and most ignored are the health issues that go un-addressed. And it's no secret that many Black Americans still don't go to the doctor, so many of these issues remain untreated, getting worse over time.

Generational curses aren't just superstition—they're inherited patterns we let run wild.

But these curses can be broken. They are all controllable, even when they don't feel like it. First, you must identify the issue. If family members keep dying from the same problems, ask yourself why. Recognize the pattern; it can help you understand how to avoid a similar fate.

Acknowledge the problem. If addiction runs in the family, ask yourself, *Am I headed down that path?* It can be tough to admit, but recognizing it as a potential issue helps you figure out how to address it and is a powerful step in breaking this curse.

Ask for help. Sometimes we can't do it alone. Asking for help shows that you realize this issue has a hold on you, and someone like an accountability partner can help steer you away from those old habits. Sometimes, it requires professional help, especially for deeply rooted issues that have been passed down through many generations.

Commit to change. Be honest and recognize how this issue has impacted your family and what you can do to improve it. Sometimes, this can even be uncomfortable or unpopular, especially if your family doesn't view the issue in the same way you do. But remember, you are now changing the legacy your family has been accustomed to, for something much better—not only for yourself, but for your current and future family as well.

Never forget: The next generation is watching you. Children learn behaviors, coping mechanisms, and belief systems from family, mostly their parents. And even when you think something is small because you're used to it, it could have a lasting impact on your family. Do you want to continue what your family has been doing? Are you ready to make a change?

For me, recognizing some of our family's patterns was both eye-opening and empowering. Especially when you realize that you are creating a better future for your family, it becomes clear that you possess the power, strength, and will to identify negativity, address it, and ultimately overcome it through conscious effort, therapy, and a commitment to creating healthier patterns for future generations. There is no need for the younger members of your family to learn about family issues and wonder if it will happen to them or if it will be "that bad."

Have patience with yourself, as some learned behaviors don't change overnight. Finally, addressing that family issue can be intimidating and scary. But it's the first step to breaking those generational curses. Breaking your family curses also allows you to see your family for who they truly are. Through the beauty and pain, they're still family, but they are human. For me, separating our family patterns from our true faith has strengthened my relationship with God. Now I realize that, while prayer is powerful, it's only effective if you put in the work.

Don't just hope for a better future—build it.

Your family's next chapter is waiting for you to act.

29

The Life and Legacy of Sam Prewitt
The Obituary That Almost Was

Dear beloved friends and family,

Today, we gather to celebrate the life and legacy of a son, brother, and friend to many, Sam Prewitt. Sam was called home to be with our Lord on Saturday, May 23, 2015. He is survived by his mother, Mrs. Prewitt; his sister Allegra; and his niece. Our hearts especially go out to his mother, who has faced the unimaginable loss of burying a husband and two children. It is painful beyond words, but though this may be hard to understand right now, we can trust that God's plan remains, even if we do not see it. In his twenty-nine years of life—brief to some, but filled with meaning—Sam made a powerful impact on this world. Mrs. Prewitt, may you find comfort in knowing that God has greeted him at the gates, saying, "Rest now, child. Your job is done. You did well."

As a child, Sam might have appeared shy—at least until you got to know him. Beneath that quiet was a one-of-a-kind spirit. Mrs. Prewitt often tells the story of how, before he could even read, Sam could identify the make and model of every car that passed by. His remarkable memory was evident early on, and his family sensed Sam was bound to be truly special.

Even with his quiet demeanor, Sam forged many enduring friendships. Relationships mattered deeply to him. While some say friends come and go, Sam never received that memo—he nurtured lifelong bonds from his earliest days in Warrensville Heights through his time at Warrensville High and Ohio Dominican University, carrying these relationships into adulthood.

Sam saw the good in everyone, giving chances when others wouldn't. He was dedicated to the community, extending kindness by welcoming new faces and ensuring that no one was left out—from introducing friends to making sure every newcomer felt at home in any room or gathering. These small acts of inclusion and kindness defined Sam and touched all of us.

When Sam entered college, he didn't just make more friends—he gained brothers. In the spring of 2006, he joined Alpha Phi Alpha fraternity, marking a transformative chapter. Fraternity life introduced Sam to a greater sense of service, brotherhood, and leadership. From college until his transition, Sam treasured his fraternal bonds and the responsibilities that came with them. Many considered him a model brother who embodied the very vision of the fraternity's founders, always ensuring his passion uplifted others and never made anyone feel excluded.

Sam never forgot a birthday, anniversary, or important milestone. This attention to the little things made his connections so genuine. He would echo any good news, making you feel seen and celebrated—even for accomplishments as small as finding your keys, which he turned into memorable mini celebrations.

Perhaps the greatest irony: Sam, the man who celebrated everyone, shied away from attention himself—even as a beloved radio personality. That, truly, was his greatest joke. His natural gift for making genuine connections served him well in his radio career as SPdaCoolKid on Power 107.5 in Columbus and Z107.9 in Cleveland. He also made his mark in digital marketing at Radio One, a testament to his unique drive and talent. Mrs. Prewitt always knew her son was special, and he proved her right.

They say the good ones die young, but that doesn't ease the pain. Still, I know Sam would be looking down and gently chiding us—he never wanted to cause anyone sadness. When you were down, Sam would find a way to get you to smile.

Let us honor Sam's memory the way he would have wanted—by cherishing the joyful moments. Recall the times Sam made you laugh. Think of your favorite memory with him. Remember the friends you met through him or the ones he befriended after your introduction. Sam excelled at turning strangers into friends, ensuring everyone ended up connected.

Think of the times you felt out of place, and remember how Sam noticed and approached to assure you weren't alone—a friend even before you realized you needed one. Sam wanted all to be friends, and that's the legacy we must uphold.

To truly honor Sam, let's carry forward his gift—make a new friend today, include someone who feels alone, and remember: Sam brought us together so that none of us would remain strangers. Let us continue his legacy of friendship and inclusivity by reaching out to someone new, just as Sam always did.

30

Plus More Life

More Life, More Legacy: The #HeartStrong
Movement Continues

Whew, that last chapter was heavy. Imagine reading your own eulogy—the emotions and the what-ifs that come with it. You get to see firsthand how people remember you: the things you said, the things you did or didn't do, the impact you made, and the way you made people feel. All your accomplishments—in career, community, and family—are on full display for friends, family, and acquaintances to remember you by. That's why what you do in the present is crucial.

Because it all leads to the end—to your legacy.

What saddens me most is knowing that if my life had ended with my heart attack, I would have missed out on some of the best parts that were still ahead. In writing my own eulogy, I was reminded that I am far from done with living and making an impact.

I wouldn't have gotten the chance to marry the love of my life, Alexis, or celebrate our wedding—one of my greatest days. The love in that room was remarkable, bringing together people from all walks of our lives. It showed me how deeply rooted our community really is.

I wouldn't have been able to travel the world. At that point, I had never crossed the Atlantic—missing the opportunity to see breathtaking places, experience new cultures and cuisines, and make new friends.

I would have missed having a front-row seat to Alexis's journey as an entrepreneur and actress. The moments spent encouraging her, cheering at her film premieres, watching her come alive in her calling—these memories would not exist.

I would have missed key moments with my family, growing closer to my mother and sister, watching my niece grow. Most of all, I would have robbed my mother of witnessing me grow into the man I am—a man who makes her proud and reminds her of my father, but with her spirit.

I would have missed time with my extended family—from the Prewitts to the Jenkinses and all of those in Northport and across the country. I would have missed getting to know my in-laws, who have accepted me as one of their own, and hearing my new nieces and nephews call me Uncle Sam.

I would never have introduced the world to King Cool, the evolved persona of my radio alter ego, SPdaCoolKid. I would not have had the opportunity to climb the corporate ladder at the nation's seventh-largest multimedia company and the largest Black-owned company. King Cool never would have lived the dream of being on the very airwaves I grew up listening to.

What strikes me now is knowing that, if my life had ended with my heart attack, I would have left a proud legacy, as chapter 29 shows, but an incomplete one. But by the grace of God, twenty-nine was not my final year. That faith I held onto carried me further than I expected, giving me the time I needed to finally put in the work. I wasn't supposed to see thirty, according to my doctors, but as my mother reminds me, "Our God is a powerful God." Ironically, in numerology, the number twenty-nine symbolizes change, progress, and ambition, self-improvement in motion. All of this converged on a Memorial Day I will never forget.

For the final time: Control the controllables.

As William Ernest Henley so boldly declares in one of my favorite poems, "Invictus": "I am the master of my fate, I am the captain of my soul." Life will always be unpredictable. It's not just about what happens to you—it's about what you do next. When adversity comes, how do you respond? How do you find your way through, or around, the challenge? Henley wrote "Invictus" while recovering from a severe illness and facing the potential amputation of one of his legs. He had already lost one leg to the same disease as a child. Throughout history, this poem has stood as a testament to indomitable spirit—the refusal to be defeated by suffering, circumstance, or fate. You are the master of your fate. You are the captain of your soul. Never forget: You have the right to make choices and to steer your own destiny. Don't let external influences or the noise of others distract you from your power to shape your own path and life.

Looking back, I realize that becoming #HeartStrong wasn't just one decision; it was built on four pillars that changed everything for me. These are the foundations of the movement we're building together:

- **Protect Your Heart and Everything in It:** Your health isn't just about you; it's about staying here for the people and passions you love.

- **Break Generational Curses:** We don't have to accept, "This is just how it is" in our families. We have the power to stop the cycle of silence and disease.

- **Control the Controllables:** You can't change your DNA, but you can change your habits, your kitchen, and your activity. Focus on what you can influence.

- **Lean on Your Tribe:** You aren't meant to do this alone. Accountability is a love language, and your community is your greatest strength.

My story is proof that when you stand on these pillars, you don't just survive—you find more life and a bigger legacy.

That starts with your relationship with food—how you view it, where you get it, how you prepare it. Learn what moderation means for you. Enjoy your childhood favorites if it's safe, or accept that some foods are simply no longer good for you. It might be hard, but it's necessary for change. Challenge yourself to cook more and design a lifestyle plan that supports your goals.

Move your body. Make sure you get physical activity—the heart and body will thank you. Whatever exercise you choose, commit to two or three sessions per week, at least thirty minutes each, and find an activity that excites you. Not only does this boost motivation and consistency, but it also improves mental health and relieves stress. I speak from experience: Working out can help save your life.

Go to the doctor. Don't avoid it. Doctors save lives and can give you more time with your family—but only if you stay active in your health care and understand your own body. Remember, you don't have to settle for the first doctor you meet; find someone you trust because you're literally trusting them with your life. Shop around, ask questions, read reviews, and make sure it feels right. Health care is personal and could shape some of the biggest decisions you ever make. Assemble a medical team that has your best interests at heart.

I admit I am not perfect. I'm still learning, and I stumble sometimes. I still fall into temptation, and that's okay. What makes my story beautiful is that it's real. You and I have been on this journey together—through highs and lows. If my story has shown you anything, I hope it's that, even when times are rough and things seem imperfect, triumph can be just around the corner.

That's why I share my #HeartStrong story—for you to know that family patterns and so-called curses have no power over how you choose to live. I want to encourage everyone, especially those living with ignored or minimized genetic ailments, to take their health seriously. Tomorrow isn't promised, so create your legacy now—one that will make you proud in the future.

Before I end, I want you to close your eyes one more time—and take a deep breath. Feel the air move through your nose, down your throat, into your lungs. Let go of all other thoughts and simply focus on your family. The people you love. Your favorite things and the people who inspire you. The ones who depend on you.

Remember those who dwell in your heart—those you fight for, those you strive to be healthy for.

Think about those who melt your stress when you're together, those who give you reason to break generational patterns, and those who keep you motivated to stay fit. Remember the ones you can't wait to see grow or with whom you long to travel the world. Consider those you've lost touch with and those you hope to reconnect with. Those you owe an apology to; those you still love, even after everything. Those you hug each day and those you hold a little longer because you know you don't always get another chance.

Now exhale fully, feeling your heartbeat soften as your body calms. When you open your eyes, remember: All those people you pictured when you breathed in and out?

Protect them.

Protect your heart.

And everything in it.

Be #HeartStrong. Always and forever.

Acknowledgements

First, I want to thank God for another day and another chance to get it right. The ancestors who continue to guide me — and our lost loved ones who we had the honor to share life with — who have since transitioned, continue to watch over and protect us.

To my mother, **Alfreda Prewitt**, and my sister, **Allegra Prewitt**, thank you for your understanding of this book's vision and mission and for truly believing in me. Shena, you told me you think I've found my calling; I received that and appreciate you saying so. In telling this story, I relived many moments from my life, and it has made me look at my mother and sister differently. Mom, thank you for raising me to be the man I am today. Your blood runs through me, cool as water, giving me patience, empathy, and understanding. The grace that I have seen you give so many is a main reason I was driven to write this book: to help people and show love to others, just as I have seen you do so many times in the past. Thank you for being my mom.

To **Em**: We may not talk every day, but I always think about you, pray for you, and forever love you. I hope one day you read this and see a different point of view.

To my Jenkins fam, who have been a major help in bringing this book to life: Shoutout to my cousin **Monita**, who was my proofreader on this project, and to my cousin **Moses**, who created my book cover. I told you I wanted something creative, and you delivered. I appreciate your vision. Even outside of the physical work, the love and support that I got from all of my Jenkins family is overwhelming. Thank you all for trusting me to tell **Bubba** and **Gussie's** story.

To the Prewitts! I love you all and appreciate you instilling that Bama pride in me! Your blood runs through me like fire, which fuels my energy, creativity, and competitiveness. Thank you all for reminding me of that every time I see you. The stories you have shared with me and the love you all show me are like no other. I hope to continue reminding you of your big brother, **Sam Edward,** and that you all smile at me just as you did at him.

To my cousin **Damita**, who helped me discover the Morrow side: Even though we don't talk every day, I thank you for the love and support you have poured into the project. Thank you!

To the many cousins on both sides of the family who donated to my book project: I appreciate you all. Thank you for believing in me.

To my "In-Loves": Thank you all for your love and support in this mission. I thank God for having an extended family that I genuinely love as much as my own.

From my Gladstone crew and Warrensville friends: I appreciate you guys for being a part of the early years of my journey. Thank you for always keeping me humble and taking me back through the memories of all the crazy games we played as kids. Most of these relationships go back over 35 years; I don't take that lightly, and I love you all for still being friends with the Kid.

To my college friends: I'm glad we made it! I hope we are all eating better now. Thank you for making my college experience unforgettable and some of the best times of my life. You all showed me what a tribe truly is, and I will never forget that. You guys are all — and always will be — family to me. ODU for life!

To my Alpha Phi Alpha brothers, especially to those with whom I had the once-in-a-lifetime honor of being initiated during our centennial year of 2006: I appreciate all you fellas and couldn't have asked for a better group to share this honor with. That goes from my hometown to my home chapter, Omicron Rho. From the charter members and big brothers to the later generations, I love and appreciate you. Our chapter is one of a kind, and I thank God for seeing me fit to be a part of it. I thank my brothers of Omicron Rho for choosing me, shaping me into the man I am today, and showing me what it's like to party hard, stay up late, and, most of all, graduate. We are still "scholars making dollas."

Thank you for allowing me passage into this fraternity of men, from whom I have learned so much and whom I consider brothers beyond blood. Thank you all for sticking with me, developing me into a leader through brotherhood, and allowing me to share those lessons with the later generations of brothers.

Even among the other Divine Nine members, I have dear, close friends in every one of these organizations; I consider some of them my best friends. The relationships we have built and the bonds that we cherish are truly special. I appreciate you all, and I am grateful to be close to so many of you. Never forget your "why," uphold your organization's values, and be an example of your organization to the best of your ability. No excuses.

To my radio family: Wow, where do we start? Whether it's RadiO-DU or Radio One, I appreciate everyone who was along this journey. To those I've learned from and those I've taught, I appreciate you for sticking in there; even when the world thinks radio is dead, you go right to work to prove otherwise. I've worked with the best from the past, in the present, and with those I can see will be great in the future. I really love watching you all work — not just those behind the mic but also those behind the scenes who make sure everything runs smoothly. I am blessed to work alongside all of you, and I am such a fan of many of your works. Nothing lasts forever, but I truly do appreciate the many years radio has allowed me to be in its space. Thank you to the game, thank you to the people, and thank you to the culture.

And I can't forget my radio supporters: I appreciate every request and every time you all ask for shoutouts. Even if you have asked for an autograph (yes, it has happened more than once!). If you have rocked with me as DJ Sammy P, DJ-SP, SPdaCoolkid, or King Cool, I truly appreciate your support. And if you know about Cool Kid Radio, now we're really talking, and you're really locked in with me! I really appreciate that!

To my Run with the Winners Crew, and especially to **Tasha**: Thank you for saving my life. Without you, this wouldn't be possible.

To the friends I met upon my return home: While I never saw myself coming back, each of you has made this one of the best decisions of my life. To those in the city who made life-changing introductions, challenged me to be better, or helped me be great, including my early readers: Thank you for your incredible feedback and love. You were instrumental in my return, reminding me every day that "Cleveland Is the Reason."

To my doctors and nurses: Thank you for saving my life so I could tell this story. Even if I was stubborn at times, I appreciate you. Let this book empower your missions in healthcare, serving as a testimony and encouragement that your patients can change.

To the American Heart Association: You have been there for every step of my journey as a survivor. Thank you for all the love, support, and opportunity to be in amazing places and spaces, all in the name of fighting heart disease and saving lives.

To all the donors of this project: Thank you so much for believing in my story and investing in me. From those whom I have known for years to those who just believe in me, thank you so much. I can't express how grateful I am for your help bringing this mission to life through this self-publishing journey.

To my editing team: Without even knowing it, you gave me confidence in my voice and kept me on track to tell this story right. Thank you for your guidance.

And to the many others I may not speak with every day: Please know I have never forgotten you. Even when you don't know it, I often think about the memories we share and look forward to bringing them up the next time I see you. Always know that I think of and pray for your well-being and health. Even though I may not pick up the phone, text, or drop a DM as much as I should, know you are close to my heart and a reason I stay #HeartStrong.

And last but not least, for the one who has my heart, my wife, **Alexis Prewitt**: I thank you for believing in me when I didn't believe in myself and for bringing me back to reality when I started to believe too much. You remind me every day why life is worth living, and I wouldn't rather do this with anybody else. Thank you for being the love and light in my life and my biggest reason to fight to be #HeartStrong. Let's continue to live this life to the fullest, travel the world, love these moments, and cherish these memories until God calls us home. And when He does, let's make sure we have plenty of stories to share with Him. I love you, Queen.

Thank you all for being a part of my journey and my tribe, watching me grow, helping me grow, and loving me through it all. It was such an honor to talk to each and every one of you from different moments in our lives.

Most importantly, to everyone reading this: Thank you for being part of the #HeartStrong movement.

References

Chapter 1

- "Heart Attack Symptoms in Women and Men." *American Heart Association.* Accessed December 24, 2025. https://www.heart.org/en/health-topics/heart-attack/symptoms-of-a-heart-attack.

- "Heart Attack." *MedlinePlus.* U.S. National Library of Medicine. Accessed December 24, 2025. https://medlineplus.gov/heartattack.html.

Chapter 2

- "Family History and Health." *National Library of Medicine.* National Institutes of Health. Accessed December 24, 2025. https://medlineplus.gov/familyhistory.html

Chapter 3

- "Hot 100: 1972 Chart Archive." *Billboard.* Accessed December 24, 2025. https://www.billboard.com/charts/hot-100/1972-01-01.

- "Shorthand Writing." *Encyclopaedia Britannica.* Accessed December 24, 2025. https://www.britannica.com/topic/shorthand.

- "Records of the Watergate Special Prosecution Force." *U.S. National Archives.* Accessed December 24, 2025. https://www.archives.gov/research/investigations/watergate.

Chapter 4

- "How Much Physical Activity Do Children Need?" *Centers for Disease Control and Prevention.* Accessed December 24, 2025. https://www.cdc.gov/physicalactivity/basics/children/index.htm.

- "Best Sandwiches in America: Cleveland's Polish Boy." *Esquire.* September 1, 2014. https://classic.esquire.com/article/2014/9/1/the-polish-boy.

- "The Best Thing I Ever Ate: Michael Symon's Favorite." *Food Network.* Accessed December 24, 2025. https://www.foodnetwork.com/shows/the-best-thing-i-ever-ate/episodes/between-bread.

Chapter 5

- "Familial Hypercholesterolemia." *MedlinePlus.* U.S. National Library of Medicine. Accessed December 24, 2025. https://medlineplus.gov/familialhypercholesterolemia.html.

- "Cholesterol Levels: What You Need to Know." *National Heart, Lung, and Blood Institute.* National Institutes of Health. Accessed December 24, 2025. https://www.nhlbi.nih.gov/health-topics/cholesterol.

- "What is Familial Hypercholesterolemia (FH)?" *Yale Medicine.* Accessed December 24, 2025. https://yalemedicine.org/conditions/familial-hypercholesterolemia/.

Chapter 7

- "Stroke Warning Signs and F.A.S.T." *American Heart Association*. Accessed December 24, 2025. https://www.heart.org/en/health-topics/stroke.

- "Family Acceptance, Stress, and Mental Health Outcomes." *AMR Therapy*. Accessed December 24, 2025. https://www.amrtherapy.com/navigating-rejection-family-conflict-impact-on-mental-health/.

- "Black and African American People's Views on Health Care." *Commonwealth Fund*. Accessed December 24, 2025. https://www.commonwealthfund.org/.

- "More Than a Program: A Culture of Women's Wellbeing at Work." *Gallup*. May 12, 2025. https://www.gallup.com/workplace/653843/program-culture-women-wellbeing-work.aspx.

- "Tracking the World's Emotional Health." *Gallup*. November 19, 2025. https://news.gallup.com/poll/695963/tracking-world-emotional-health.aspx.

- "Worry and Stress Worldwide: Global Rise in Mental Health Struggles." *Gallup News*. Accessed December 24, 2025. https://www.gallup.com/analytics/349262/gallup-global-emotions-report.aspx.

- "Silent Stroke." *MedlinePlus*. U.S. National Library of Medicine. Accessed December 24, 2025. https://medlineplus.gov/silentstroke.html.

- "Internet Use Became the Norm for Humanity Only Very

Recently." *Our World in Data.* Accessed December 24, 2025. https://ourworldindata.org/data-insights/internet-use-became-the-norm-for-humanity-only-very-recently

Chapter 8
- "Stress and Healthful Eating." *Johns Hopkins Medicine.* Accessed December 24, 2025. https://hub.jhu.edu/at-work/2021/08/13/stress-and-healthful-eating/

Chapter 9
- "Grief and Loss: Coping Tips." *American Psychological Association.* Accessed December 24, 2025. https://www.apa.org/topics/families/grief.

- "Vices as Coping Mechanisms." *Smart Counseling and Mental Health Center.* Accessed December 24, 2025. https://www.smartcounselingca.com/blog/vices-as-coping-mechanisms.

- "Long-Term Effects of Chronic Stress and Family Burden." *Gallup News.* Accessed December 24, 2025. https://news.gallup.com/poll/145455/Family-Caregivers-Feeling-Strain.aspx.

- "Beyond the surface: Unmasking the ubiquity of Trauma Normalization." *Millennium Journal of Health.* Accessed December 24, 2025. https://mjh.sphmmc.edu.et/MJH_VOLUME_3_1_2024/Editorial%20MJH-vol%203(1).pdf

- "Mental Structures and the Normalization of Trauma." *Millennium Journal of Health.* Accessed December 24, 2025. https://www.healthaffairs.org/doi/10.1377/hlthaff.2021.01466.

- "Frequently Asked Questions About Hospice Care."

National Institute on Aging. Accessed December 24, 2025. https://www.nia.nih.gov/health/hospice-and-palliative-care/frequently-asked-questions-about-hospice-care.

Chapter 10

- "LDL and HDL Cholesterol: What You Need to Know." *Centers for Disease Control and Prevention.* Accessed December 24, 2025. https://www.cdc.gov/cholesterol/ldl_hdl.htm.

- "The Most American City in America." *The Atlantic.* Accessed December 24, 2025. https://www.theatlantic.com/business/archive/2015/05/the-most-american-city-in-america/393278/.

- "McGriddle Breakfast Sandwiches Return." *McDonald's Corporation.* Press release, 2003. https://news.mcdonalds.com/.

- *Ohio Dominican University.* "At a Glance: About ODU." Accessed December 24, 2025. https://www.ohiodominican.edu/.

- "Income, Poverty, and Health Insurance Coverage in the United States: 2008." *U.S. Census Bureau.* Accessed December 24, 2025. https://www.census.gov/library/publications/2009/demo/p60-236.html.

- *Dietary Guidelines for Americans, 2020–2025. U.S. Department of Agriculture.* Accessed December 24, 2025. https://www.dietaryguidelines.gov/.

- "Sodium in Your Diet." *U.S. Food and Drug Administration.* March 5, 2024. Accessed December 24, 2025. https://www.fda.gov/food/nutrition-education-resources-materials/sodium-your-diet.

- "Monitoring micronutrient status in populations." *World Health Organization.* Accessed December 24, 2025. https://www.who.int/activities/monitoring-micronutrient-status-in-populations.

Chapter 12

- "Examples of Bad Bedside Manner Versus Medical Malpractice." *Freedland Harwin Gander Valori* blog. Accessed December 24, 2025. www.fhvlegal.com/blog/examples-of-bad-bedside-manner-versus-medical-malpractice.

- Penner, L. A., et al. "Aversive Racism and Medical Interactions with Black Patients." *Journal of Social Issues* 70, no. 2 (2014). https://pmc.ncbi.nlm.nih.gov/articles/PMC2835170.

- Shen, M. J., E. B. Peterson, R. Costas-Muñiz, M. H. Hernandez, S. T. Jewell, K. Matsoukas, and C. L. Bylund. "The Effects of Race and Racial Concordance on Patient-Physician Communication: A Systematic Review of the Literature." *Journal of Racial and Ethnic Health Disparities* 5, no. 1 (2018): 117–140. https://doi.org/10.1007/s40615-017-0350-4.

Chapter 13

- "Healthy Eating." *American Heart Association.* Accessed December 24, 2025. https://www.heart.org/en/healthy-living/healthy-eating.

- "Diabetes and Cultural Foods." *Centers for Disease Control and Prevention.* Accessed December 24, 2025. https://www.cdc.gov/diabetes/healthy-eating/diabetes-cultural-foods.html.

- "Fats and Cholesterol." *The Nutrition Source,* Harvard T.

H. Chan School of Public Health. Accessed December 24, 2025. https://nutritionsource.hsph.harvard.edu/what-shoul d-you-eat/fats-and-cholesterol/.

- "Americans' Challenges with Health Care Costs." *Kaiser Family Foundation*. July 11, 2025. https://www.kff.org/health-costs/a mericans-challenges-with-health-care-costs/.

Chapter 15

- "Healthy Eating for a Healthy Weight." *Centers for Disease Control and Prevention*. Accessed December 24, 2025. https://www .cdc.gov/healthy-weight-growth/healthy-eating/index.html.

- "Preeclampsia." *Johns Hopkins Medicine*. Accessed December 24, 2025. https://www.hopkinsmedicine.org/health/conditio ns-and-diseases/preeclampsia.

- "Grief and Coping: Vices as Avoidance Mechanisms." *Smart Counseling and Mental Health Center*. Accessed December 24, 2025.

Chapter 16

- "Death rates linked to obesity-related heart disease are up, especially among men." *American Heart Association*. Accessed December 24, 2025. https://www.heart.org/en/news/2024/11/13/death-rate s-linked-to-obesity-related-heart-disease-are-up.

- "LeBron: I'm Coming Back to Cleveland." *Sports Illustrated*. July 11, 2014. https://www.si.com/nba/2014/07/11/lebron-james-c leveland-cavaliers.

- "Census 2020: Cleveland City Planning Commission." *City of Cleveland Planning Commission*. Accessed December 24, 2025. https://planning.clevelandohio.gov/census2020/index.html.

Chapter 17

- "Walking vs. Running: Which Form of Cardio Has Better Health Benefits?" *American Council on Exercise*. Accessed December 24, 2025. https://www.acefitness.org/about-ace/press-room/in-the-news/8287/walking-vs-running-which-form-of-cardio-has-better-health-benefits/.

- Nike. "Building Consistency and Motivation." *Nike Run Club*. Mobile app. Accessed December 24, 2025.

Chapter 18

- FAIR Health Releases Study on Ground Ambulance Services." *FAIR Health*. Accessed December 24, 2025. https://www.fairhealth.org/article/fair-health-releases-study-on-ground-ambulance-services.

- "Tips to Handle Running in Hot Weather." Health Essentials, *Cleveland Clinic*. Accessed December 24, 2025. https://health.clevelandclinic.org/running-in-the-heat-tips-to-handle-hot-weather-while-getting-in-your-miles.

- "Shortness of Breath: Causes." *Mayo Clinic*. Accessed December 24, 2025. https://www.mayoclinic.org/symptoms/shortness-of-breath/basics/causes/sym-20050890.

- "REM Sleep Behavior Disorder: An Early Warning Sign for Neurodegeneration." *Sleep Medicine Clinics*. ScienceDirect. Accessed December 24, 2025. https://www.sciencedirect.com/topics/neuroscience/rem-sleep-behavior-disorder.

Chapter 19

- "Warning Signs of a Heart Attack." *American Heart Association.* Accessed December 24, 2025. https://www.heart.org/en/health-topics/heart-attack/warning-signs-of-a-heart-attack.

- "4 Side Effects of Dehydration." *Baptist Health.* Accessed December 24, 2025. https://www.baptisthealth.com/blog/health-and-wellness/4-side-effects-of-dehydration-on-the-human-body.

- "High Cholesterol Facts." *Centers for Disease Control and Prevention.* Accessed December 24, 2025. https://www.cdc.gov/cholesterol/data-research/facts-stats/index.html.

- "Average Ambulance Costs." *Kaiser Family Foundation* and *FairHealthConsumer.org.* Accessed December 24, 2025. https://www.fairhealth.org/article/fair-health-releases-study-on-ground-ambulance-services.

- "Cardiac catheterization." Mayo Clinic. Accessed December 24, 2025. https://www.mayoclinic.org/tests-procedures/cardiac-catheterization/about/pac-20384695.

Chapter 20

- "Cardiac rehabilitation." *Mayo Clinic.* Accessed December 24, 2025. https://www.mayoclinic.org/tests-procedures/cardiac-rehabilitation/about/pac-20385192.

- "Final Determination Regarding Partially Hydrogenated Oils."

U.S. Food and Drug Administration. Accessed December 24, 2025. https://www.fda.gov/food/food-additives-petitions/final-determination-regarding-partially-hydrogenated-oils-removing-trans-fat.

- "REPLACE: Trans Fat-Free." *World Health Organization.* Accessed December 24, 2025. https://www.who.int/teams/nutrition-and-food-safety/replace-trans-fat.

- "Trans Fat." *World Health Organization.* Fact sheet. Accessed December 23, 2025. https://www.who.int/news-room/fact-sheets/detail/trans-fat.

- "The Skinny on Fats." *American Heart Association.* Accessed December 24, 2025. https://www.heart.org/en/health-topics/cholesterol/prevention-and-treatment-of-high-cholesterol-hyperlipidemia/the-skinny-on-fats.

Chapter 21

- "Manipulation Under Anesthesia." *OrthoInfo*, American Academy of Orthopaedic Surgeons. Accessed December 24, 2025. https://orthoinfo.aaos.org/en/treatment/manipulation-under-anesthesia-for-total-knee-arthroplasty/.

- "Trans Fat." *American Heart Association.* Accessed December 24, 2025. https://www.heart.org/en/healthy-living/healthy-eating/eat-smart/fats/trans-fat.

- "Physical Activity Basics." *Centers for Disease Control and Prevention.* Accessed December 24, 2025. https://www.cdc.gov/p

hysical-activity-basics/guidelines/index.html.

- Frankl, Viktor E. *Man's Search for Meaning.* Boston: Beacon Press, 2006.

- "Stop comparing yourself to others." *Harvard Health Publishing*, Harvard Medical School. Accessed December 24, 2025. https://www.health.harvard.edu/mental-health/stop-comparing-yourself-to-others.

- "What is a Scar?" *Johns Hopkins Medicine.* Accessed December 24, 2025. https://www.hopkinsmedicine.org/health/conditions-and-diseases/scars.

- "Exercise: 7 benefits of regular physical activity." *Mayo Clinic.* Accessed December 24, 2025. https://www.mayoclinic.org/healthy-lifestyle/fitness/in-depth/exercise/art-20048389.

- "Patellar tendon tear." *Mayo Clinic.* Accessed December 24, 2025. https://www.mayoclinic.org/diseases-conditions/patellar-tendon-tear/diagnosis-treatment/drc-20353243.

- "Chronic Illness and Mental Health: Recognizing and Treating Depression." *National Institute of Mental Health.* Accessed December 24, 2025. https://www.nimh.nih.gov/health/publications/chronic-illness-mental-health.

- "Health benefits of cycling: a systematic review." *National Institutes of Health (PubMed).* Accessed December 24, 2025. https://pubmed.ncbi.nlm.nih.gov/21496106/.

- "Irregular sleep patterns may raise risk of

heart disease." *NIH Research Matters*, National Institutes of Health. Accessed December 24, 2025. https://www.nih.gov/news-events/nih-research-matters/irregular-sleep-patterns-may-raise-risk-heart-disease.

Chapter 23

- "Why walking is the most underrated form of exercise." *NBC News*. Accessed December 24, 2025. https://www.nbcnews.com/better/health/why-walking-most-underrated-form-exercise-ncna797271.

- "Using the SMART-EST Goals in Lifestyle Medicine Prescription." *National Institutes of Health (PubMed Central)*. Accessed December 24, 2025. https://pmc.ncbi.nlm.nih.gov/articles/PMC7232896/.

Chapter 24

- "2018 Guideline on the Management of Blood Cholesterol." *American College of Cardiology/American Heart Association*. Accessed December 24, 2025. https://www.ahajournals.org/doi/10.1161/CIR.0000000000000625.

- "PCSK9 Inhibitors." *American Heart Association*. Accessed December 24, 2025. https://www.heart.org/en/health-topics/cholesterol/prevention-and-treatment-of-high-cholesterol-hyperlipidemia/pcsk9-inhibitors.

- "Cholesterol." *Centers for Disease Control and Prevention*. Accessed December 24, 2025. https://www.cdc.gov/cholesterol/index.html.

Chapter 25

- "Talking with Your Doctor." *MedlinePlus*, National Library of Medicine. Accessed December 24, 2025. https://medlineplus.gov/talkingwithyourdoctor.html.

- "Patient Rights." *American Medical Association*. Accessed December 24, 2025. https://www.ama-assn.org/delivering-care/ethics/patient-rights.

- "Impact of Communication in Healthcare." *Institute for Healthcare Communication*. Accessed December 24, 2025. https://healthcarecomm.org/about-us/impact-of-communication-in-healthcare/.

- "The Role of Emotion and Communication in Medical Encounters." *Journal of Patient Experience* 4, no. 4 (2017): 165–167. Accessed December 24, 2025. https://doi.org/10.1177/2374373517714450.

- Mercer, S. W., and W. J. Reynolds. "Empathy and Quality of Care." *British Journal of General Practice* 52, suppl. (2002): S9-12. Accessed December 24, 2025. https://www.ncbi.nlm.nih.gov/pmc/articles/PMC1316134/.

- "Chronic Illness and Mental Health: Recognizing and Treating Depression." *National Institute of Mental Health*. Accessed December 24, 2025. https://www.nimh.nih.gov/health/publications/chronic-illness-mental-health.

Chapter 26

- "Air Fryers: Are They Healthy?" *Cleveland Clinic*. Accessed December 24, 2025. https://health.clevelandclinic.org/air-fryer

-healthy.

- "The truth about fast food." *Harvard Health Publishing*, Harvard Medical School. Accessed December 24, 2025. https://www.health.harvard.edu/staying-healthy/the-truth-about-fast-food.

- "Monosodium glutamate (MSG): Is it harmful?" *Mayo Clinic*. Accessed December 24, 2025. https://www.mayoclinic.org/healthy-lifestyle/nutrition-and-healthy-eating/expert-answers/monosodium-glutamate/faq-20058196.

- "How To Use the Nutrition Facts Label." *National Heart, Lung, and Blood Institute*. Accessed December 24, 2025. https://www.nhlbi.nih.gov/health/heart-healthy-living/healthy-eating/nutrition-label.

- "Substances Added to Food." *U.S. Food and Drug Administration*. Accessed December 24, 2025. https://www.cfsanappsexternal.fda.gov/scripts/fdcc/index.cfm?set=FoodSubstances.

Chapter 27
- Airhihenbuwa, Collins O., and Shiriki K. Kumanyika. "Cultural Aspects of African American Eating Patterns." *Ethnicity & Health* 1, no. 3 (1996): 245–260. https://www.tandfonline.com/doi/abs/10.1080/13557858.1996.9961793.

- "The importance of portion control." *Harvard Health Publishing*, Harvard Medical School. Accessed December 24, 2025. https://www.health.harvard.edu/diet-and-weight-loss/the-importance-of-portion-control.

- "Portion Size and Overeating: Understanding the Connection." *National Institutes of Health (PubMed)*. Accessed December 24, 2025. https://pubmed.ncbi.nlm.nih.gov/24341331/.

- Oliver, J. Eric. *Fat Politics: The Real Story Behind America's Obesity Epidemic*. New York: Oxford University Press, 2006.

- "Herd Mentality: Are We Programmed to Follow the Crowd?" *Psychology Today*. Accessed December 24, 2025. https://www.psychologytoday.com/us/basics/herd-mentality.

Chapter 28

- "Life's Essential 8: Your checklist for lifelong good health." *American Heart Association*. Accessed December 24, 2025. https://www.heart.org/en/healthy-living/healthy-lifestyle/lifes-essential-8.

- Clarke, Steve, Justin Oakley, Jonathan Pugh, and Dominic Wilkinson. "Misaligned Hope and Conviction in Health Care." *Bioethics* 39, no. 3 (2025): 232–239. https://pmc.ncbi.nlm.nih.gov/articles/PMC11831707/.

- "How habits in your 20s shape your heart for life." *Harvard Gazette*, Harvard University. Accessed December 24, 2025. https://news.harvard.edu/gazette/story/2025/11/how-habits-in-your-20s-shape-your-heart-for-life/.

- "Heart disease - Diagnosis and treatment." *Mayo Clinic*. Accessed December 24, 2025. https://www.mayoclinic.org/diseases-conditions/heart-disease/diagnosis-treatment/drc-20353124.

- Songy, David. "Spiritualizing: An Unhelpful Defense Mechanism." *SLIconnect*, Saint Luke Institute. Accessed December 24, 2025. https://www.sliconnect.org/spiritualizing-an-unhelpful-defense-mechanism/.

Chapter 30

- Henley, William Ernest. "Invictus." *Poetry Foundation*. Accessed December 24, 2025. https://www.poetryfoundation.org/poems/51642/invictus.

About the author

Sam "SP" Prewitt is a 20+ year media veteran, community leader, and the voice of "King Cool" on Cleveland's 93.1 WZAK. He has spent his career connecting with audiences through music, culture, and conversation, but in 2015 the conversation changed.

On Memorial Day weekend, at just 29 years old, Sam suffered a massive heart attack—a wake-up call that stripped away his denial and forced him to confront the silent killers of stress and genetic history. He didn't just survive; he rebuilt his life with a new purpose: to help others *Protect Your Heart and Everything In It.*

Today, Sam is a leading voice in the #HeartStrong movement. He serves on the board of the Greater Cleveland American Heart Association and on its national Communications and Marketing Coordinating Committee, blending high-level expertise with a personal mission to break the silence around men's health and genetic risks.

A proud graduate of Ohio Dominican University and a native of Cleveland, OH, Sam lives his mission every day—whether he's cycling through the city to promote active living, cherishing moments with his wife Alexis, or sharing his journey to help you save your own life.